Extended Essay

Skills for Success

Paul Hoang
Chris Taylor

Authors' acknowledgements

Paul Hoang – Dedicated to David Cottam, John Nixon and Marc Morris – thank you for opening so many doors of opportunities for me whilst you were Principal of Sha Tin College.

Chris Taylor – To all my Hong Kong IB students; past, present and future.

Hachette UK's policy is to use papers that are natural, renewable and recyclable products and made from wood grown in sustainable forests. The logging and manufacturing processes are expected to conform to the environmental regulations of the country of origin.

Orders: please contact Bookpoint Ltd, 130 Park Drive, Milton Park, Abingdon, Oxon OX14 4SE. Telephone: (44) 01235 827720. Fax: (44) 01235 400454. Email education@bookpoint.co.uk Lines are open from 9 a.m. to 5 p.m., Monday to Saturday, with a 24-hour message answering service. You can also order through our website: www.hoddereducation.com

This work has been developed independently from and is not endorsed by the International Baccalaureate (IB).

ISBN: 9781510415126

© Paul Hoang and Chris Taylor 2017

First published in 2017 by

Hodder Education,

An Hachette UK Company

Carmelite House

50 Victoria Embankment

London EC4Y 0DZ

www.hoddereducation.com

Impression number   10 9 8 7 6 5 4 3 2

Year   2021 2020 2019 2018 2017

Cover photo © Le Moal Olivier /123RF.com

Illustrations by Richard Duszczak and Aptara

Typeset Aptara, Inc.

Printed in Spain

A catalogue record for this title is available from the British Library.

Contents

Introduction

How to use this book

Welcome to the Extended Essay (EE) for the IB Diploma: Skills for Success.

This guide will help prepare you for your EE in an efficient and logical way. Each chapter of the book looks at a different aspect of the essay in detail, while practice exercises are also included to help you check your understanding.

To ensure students aim for their best grade in the EE this guide:

- Includes an opening infographics spread in each chapter
- Builds skills for success through a range of strategies and detailed expert advice, such as formulating good research questions
- Covers all the IB requirements with clear and concise explanations, such as the assessment criteria and rules on academic honesty
- Demonstrates what is required to get the best grade
- Adds reference to the IB Learner Profile.

Key features of this guide include:

EXPERT TIP

These tips appear throughout the book and provide guidance on steps you can take and key things you should consider in order to help you boost your final grade.

COMMON MISTAKE

Potential pitfalls are highlighted for students in each chapter, in the form of 'Common mistakes'. Watch out for these!

EXAMPLE TASK

In some chapters a number of short tasks are included. These tasks give you the opportunity to apply the knowledge of the chapter in example situations, reinforcing your learning and further preparing you for your EE.

CHAPTER SUMMARY KEY POINTS

At the end of each chapter key knowledge is distilled in to a short checklist to help you review everything you've learnt over the previous pages.

■ END OF CHAPTER QUIZ

At the end of each chapter a short quiz is included to test the knowledge you have learnt and help you consolidate your understanding.

Aims of the Extended Essay

The EE aims to provide students with the opportunity to:

- Engage and pursue independent academic research on a focused topic within the chosen IB subject
- Carry out in-depth research in an area of personal interest
- Develop the ATL skills of research, thinking, self-management and communication
- Develop creative and critical thinking skills
- Experience the excitement and rewards of intellectual discovery
- Reflect on the research, writing and learning process.

Overview of the Extended Essay

- The EE is part of the compulsory core for all IB Diploma Programme students.
- It requires approximately 40 hours of work by the student.
- It involves three to five hours of supervision with each student.
- There are three mandatory reflection sessions, including a final *viva voce*.
- Candidates must anonymize their essay; instead of using their name or candidate number, the personal code (for example, nqh510) should be used.
- The essay is marked out of **34** (criterion-based assessment), based on five grade bands:
  - □ Grade A = The essay is of an excellent standard
  - □ Grade B = The essay is of a good standard
  - □ Grade C = The essay is of a satisfactory standard
  - □ Grade D = The essay is of a mediocre standard
  - □ Grade E = The essay is of an elementary standard.
- The EE is externally marked by an IB examiner using five assessment criteria:
  - □ Criterion A = Focus and method (6 marks)
  - □ Criterion B = Knowledge and understanding (6 marks)
  - □ Criterion C = Critical thinking (12 marks)
  - □ Criterion D = Formal presentation (4 marks)
  - □ Criterion E = Engagement (6 marks).

About the authors

Paul Hoang is Vice Principal and IB Diploma Programme Coordinator at Sha Tin College, English Schools Foundation in Hong Kong. He is a member of the editorial board for *IB Review,* Philip Allan's flagship publication for the IB. Paul is the author of several publications including *Economics for the IB Diploma Revision Guide* (Hodder Education), *IB Business Management, 3rd edn* (IBID Press), *IGCSE Business Studies for Edexcel* (Anforme), and *Cambridge IGCSE and O Level Economics* (Hodder Education). He is an experienced IB examiner and has over 10 years of experience as an IB Workshop Leader.

Chris Taylor is Extended Essay Coordinator at Sha Tin College – an international school and IB World School with over 1,200 students. He teaches IB History and has examined the EE component of the Diploma for over 10 years. Chris authored *Riding the Dragon* (CreateSpace), a book that details his visits to every province in China and the culture, history and people in each of these. He is a regular contributing author of *IB Review* magazine, specializing in IB History and the Extended Essay. Chris is also a travel writer for the *South China Morning Post*, Hong Kong's leading English-language newspaper.

Criterion A

Focus and method (6 marks)

Topic: Is your topic communicated accurately and effectively? Are the purpose and focus of your research clear and appropriate?

Research question: Is your research question clearly stated and focused (your research question must be a question, with a question mark)? Does your completed essay continuously relate to your research question, or have you been sidetracked? Many essays lose marks by not sticking to the question.

Methodology: How are you going to carry out your research? How will you analyze and show your findings? Has an appropriate range of relevant source(s) and/or method(s) been selected and used in relation to your topic and research question?

Criterion B

Knowledge and understanding (6 marks)

Context: Is your selection of source materials relevant and appropriate to the research question?

Subject-specific terminology and concepts: Is your knowledge of the topic clear and coherent and are your sources used effectively and with understanding?

assessment criteria

Criterion C

Critical thinking (12 marks)

Research: Is your research appropriate and relevant to your research question?

Analysis of your research: How deep was your analysis? Is your research analyzed effectively and clearly focused on the research question?

Discussion and evaluation: Is your argument reasoned, effective and focused, and developed from your research? Is your conclusion consistent with your argument? If it is a good one, it may throw up other questions.

Criterion D

Formal presentation (4 marks)

Structure: The way in which your essay is constructed. Is your essay laid out in the conventional way expected of such essays?

Layout: Is your essay set out according to the IB's Extended Essay equirements? (For example: Are your pages numbered? Have you used a 12-point, readable font that is double spaced?)

Criterion E

Engagement (6 marks)

This criterion assesses your completed Reflections on Planning and Progress Form (RPPF) through a focus on the writing process:

- How thoroughly have you considered ideas and actions in response to setbacks experienced in your research process?
- Do your reflections show intellectual and personal engagement?

1 Understanding the assessment criteria

The new assessment criteria

The assessment criteria for the Extended Essay (EE) have been radically changed and reduced from 11 criteria to just five. The number of total marks has been reduced from 36 to 34. The new criteria are designed to be accessible to all candidates and to reward essays of a wide variety of standards (though scoring an 'E' grade for the essay is still a failing condition for the entire IB Diploma).

Overall, the new assessment criteria are applied more holistically throughout the essay. One exception is the final criterion, which is designed to assess your ability to reflect meaningfully on the process of researching and writing the EE, and your *engagement* with the essay.

Examiners will use the 'best-fit' method of awarding the different mark bands for each assessment criterion. Advice on how to show evidence of critical thinking in your EE is given in Chapter 8.

The new assessment criteria

Criterion A	Focus and method
Criterion B	Knowledge and understanding
Criterion C	Critical thinking
Criterion D	Formal presentation
Criterion E	Engagement

> **EXPERT TIP**
>
> As you write your EE, ensure you have maintained focus on your research question throughout the essay. You should do this explicitly by linking your work to the research question at various points throughout, including in your conclusion.

The assessment criteria, one-by-one

Criterion A

Focus and method (6 marks)

This criterion requires you to ensure that your topic is communicated accurately and effectively and the purpose and focus of your research are clear and appropriate. Your research question should be clearly stated and focused. Remember, your research question must be a question, ending with a question mark.

Criterion A also considers methodology, that is, how you are going to carry out your research, and how you intend to analyze and show your findings. Your essay must continuously relate to your research question and you should avoid getting side-tracked. Many essays lose marks because the writer does not stick to addressing the research question.

To score a good mark on this criterion you have to use an appropriate range of relevant sources and methods, such as subject-specific tools, theories and techniques. These must be used in relation to your chosen topic and research question.

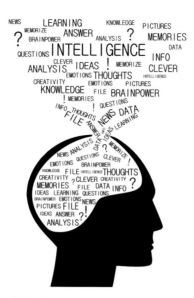

Critical thinking involves a variety of analytical and evaluative skills

It is vital to retain a clear focus on your research question throughout your essay

Criterion B

Knowledge and understanding (6 marks)

Your selection of source materials must be relevant and appropriate to the research question. Also your knowledge of the chosen topic should be clear and coherent.

It is important to use specialist terminology and concepts in an accurate, appropriate and consistent way throughout the EE. Your supporting source materials from your secondary research should be selected wisely so that these can be used effectively and purposefully in answering the research question.

This assessment criterion also assesses your ability to articulate your ideas and arguments. Hence, the precise and correct use of subject-specific language is important in all essays, not just language and literature essays.

> **EXPERT TIP**
>
> Show evidence of your knowledge and understanding of subject **content** and **concepts** throughout the essay by defining or explaining them clearly in the **context** of your research question.

Criterion C

Critical thinking (12 marks)

> **EXPERT TIP**
>
> To critically analyze effectively, think **RED**:
>
> **R** – Recognize assumptions
>
> **E** – Evaluate arguments
>
> **D** – Draw conclusions

There is now a greater focus on critical thinking, with this criterion being worth over one-third of the total marks for the EE. In order to be able to demonstrate critical thinking when analysing sources you must have a deep understanding of subject-specific terminology, theories and concepts. Therefore, wherever possible, it makes sense for you to be studying your choice of EE subject at Higher Level.

For Criterion C you need to consider the extent to which your research is appropriate and relevant to your research question. For example:

- How reliable were your research findings?
- How deep was your analysis?

- Is your research analyzed effectively and focused clearly on the research question?
- Is your argument well-reasoned and clearly developed from your research?
- Is your conclusion consistent with your argument? Does it throw up any other questions to be answered outside of the scope of your essay's conclusions?

Secondary research is required in an EE for *all* subjects, and you will need to show the examiner your ability to engage with sources in a critical way. A review of academic sources related to your topic is necessary, while alternative viewpoints from academics or other sources with expertise in your chosen topic will help you to critically evaluate your own arguments. Challenging your personal stance on the question, by considering opposing perspectives of others, is one aspect of being an effective critical thinker.

A good essay will rely on well-researched and specific-subject knowledge

Deal with your sources critically rather than accepting them at face value

You must show evidence of critical engagement throughout the essay by analysing and evaluating the data, materials and sources you have used. Moreover, ensure your discussion links explicitly to the research question and the sources of data cited.

See Chapter 8 for further details of showing evidence of critical thinking in your EE.

COMMON MISTAKE

Students often think that evaluation and evidence of critical thinking should appear in a separate paragraph at the end of their essays. In fact, the best evaluation is integrated into the arguments presented throughout an essay, instead of being placed as an isolated section of the essay.

▪ Criterion D

▪ Formal presentation (4 marks)

This criterion concerns the way in which your essay is constructed. For example, does your EE follow the conventions of an academic essay, and conform to the IB's stated requirements?

There are clear guidelines for the presentation of your essay, including the use of an acceptable font, font size, line spacing and file type (for electronic uploading). You are also expected to use a system of referencing throughout the essay, in a systematic and consistent way. It is advisable that you use a recognized style for citations and referencing (see Chapter 5 for further guidance). Failure to follow the guidelines will cost you valuable marks unnecessarily.

Reflection is a key component of the Extended Essay

In particular, pay attention to the format of the EE. Your essay should contain the following elements:

- Title page
- Contents page
- Main body
- Conclusion(s)
- Quotations that are correctly cited and referenced
- Tables and illustrations, where appropriate (but these should be directly related to the text and be fully acknowledged)
- Bibliography of all works cited
- Appendices where appropriate (though be aware that the examiner is not obliged to read these)
- A completed Reflections on Planning and Progress Form (RPPF). See Chapter 7 for more details on this.

> **EXPERT TIP**
>
> Students are encouraged to use a Researcher's Reflection Space (RRS) to help with their reflections. This is particularly important if you are writing a World Studies Extended Essay (WSEE). The RRS can take any suitable form, such as an illustration, journal entries or even an online blog. Your personal opinions, feelings, values and other comments in relation to the research and topic being studied can be recorded in the RRS. See Chapter 7 for further details about using the RRS.

In addition, there are very clear rules about the word count and formatting of the essay and these must be closely adhered to. See Chapter 3 for further details of the formal requirements for presentation of the EE.

Criterion E

Engagement (6 marks)

This criterion assesses your completed RPPF. Reflections could include your thoughts on questions, such as:

- How did you arrive at the approach and strategies chosen?
- How thoroughly have you considered ideas and actions in response to setbacks experienced in the research and writing process?
- Do your reflections show intellectual and personal engagement?
- How has your understanding developed or changed as a result of your research and findings?
- Are there any questions that emerged following from your research?
- How have you developed as an IB learner?

Your personal engagement with the Extended Engagement is assessed via the three compulsory reflections you write on the RPPF. A maximum of 500 words (in total for the three reflections) should complement your essay and allow your own voice to come through. These reflections must highlight what you are thinking, planning or reviewing at three different stages of the process.

Chapter 7 looks at the requirements for reflection in the EE in much more detail.

■ Subject-specific guidelines

The criterion outlines you have just read are generic guidelines on how to interpret the assessment criteria for all EEs. Make sure you also read the advice given in the IB *Extended Essay Guide* about the assessment criteria specific to your chosen subject. You should then discuss this with your EE supervisor to help you to better understand each assessment criterion in the context of your chosen topic.

> **EXPERT TIP**
>
> The IB recommends that an EE supervisor spends a minimum of three hours, and a maximum of five hours, with each candidate. You should make the most of this opportunity, not only to gain advice and feedback but also to demonstrate your level of engagement in the whole process of producing your EE.

Examiners will adopt a 'best-fit' model when they mark your essay

The Internal Assessment (IA) and EE are distinct and different components. Do not assume that what is acceptable for an IA is permissible for an EE, even within the same subject. For example, primary research collection is expected in the Higher Level Business Management IA, but this is not a requirement in the EE. Reading the EE report for your subject would also help you to avoid making any self-penalizing mistakes.

> **EXPERT TIP**
>
> Criteria D and E alone are worth almost 30% of the available marks and there should be no reason to lose (m)any of these marks!

The 'best-fit' approach

Examiners are instructed to use a 'best-fit' approach in the assessment of your EE. The IB uses mark bands (for example, 1–2 marks, 3–4 marks) to judge the level of your responses and examiners assess your EE using the different mark bands for each assessment criterion. Using the best-fit model allows examiners to use their judgement in crediting you for what is in your essay, instead of penalizing you for what is missing.

The aim of the best-fit approach is to find the level descriptor that most accurately conveys your level of attainment. It means that the mark you are awarded (for each assessment criterion) is the one that most fairly reflects the balance of achievement against the mark band. It is not necessary for every indicator of a level descriptor to be met for that mark to be awarded. The examiner will use their professional judgement to credit you for what is there in the essay.

You can gain the highest level mark descriptor for each assessment criterion without a faultless essay. Examiners are instructed to mark positively and to award the highest levels where appropriate – this is good news for you as a candidate!

Grade descriptors for the Extended Essay

■ A – Work of an excellent standard

For a grade A, you are expected to have a personal and conceptual approach to the EE. You will also have documented all the key decisions made, in detail through the writing of the EE. There is particular attention paid to **reflections** to gauge the level of engagement in the whole process.

■ B – Work of a good standard

This grade requires a clear engagement with the essay through key decision-making and reflections. You will have demonstrated appropriate research skills in order to address the research question. There is also reasonable application of source materials and subject content, concepts and context. Your conclusion will be consistent with the analysis and evidence provided.

■ C – Work of a satisfactory standard

For a C grade, you will have provided evidence of engagement but your essay and decision-making will be mostly based on factual information. The work is likely to be descriptive rather than analytical. Your reflections will not be personal but more concerned with procedures and processes. There may be some concerns about the presentation and structure of your essay.

■ D – Work of a mediocre standard

For a grade D the engagement is likely to be superficial and the reflection entirely narrative and/or procedural. The work demonstrates a lack of research, perhaps due to a lack of focus on the research question. There will be inconsistencies, irrelevancies and inaccuracies in the work presented. The format and structure of the essay may be difficult to follow.

■ E – Work of an elementary standard

An E grade suggests the student has shown very limited factual or focused decision-making. The approach taken is unsystematic and subject-specific knowledge is limited or partially accurate. There is no or very limited personal reflection or engagement in the process. **Remember that an E grade in the EE is a failing condition for the whole IB Diploma.**

Awareness of the grade descriptors will help to turn an essay from 'mediocre' to 'excellent'

For a summary of the assessment of the EE, have a look at this poster from *IB Review* magazine: **goo.gl/PZ4ldv**

You might want to print it off and pin it somewhere useful so that you can consult it regularly as you write your EE.

CHAPTER SUMMARY KEY POINTS

- The number of assessment criteria for the EE has been reduced from 11 to five.

- The assessment criteria are applied more holistically, meaning evidence of each criterion should be shown *throughout* the whole essay.

- The criterion that is worth the most marks is Criterion C (critical thinking) – worth 12 marks out of 34.

- Criterion D, worth six marks, is concerned with the formal presentation of the essay.

- An E grade in the EE is still a failing condition for the whole IB Diploma.

- You are required to record your reflections (of the whole EE process) on the Reflections on Planning and Progress Form (RPPF). There is a maximum 500 words allowed on the RPPF.

- Examiners will mark your EE using the 'best-fit' model – you will be credited for what is in your essay, instead of being penalized for what is missing.

- The best-fit approach means that it is not necessary for every indicator of a grade descriptor to be met for that mark band to be awarded.

- The assessment criteria and maximum marks per criterion are shown in the table below.

Criterion A	Focus and method	6 marks
Criterion B	Knowledge and understanding	6 marks
Criterion C	Critical thinking	12 marks
Criterion D	Formal presentation	4 marks
Criterion E	Engagement	6 marks

■ END OF CHAPTER QUIZ

	Question	True	False
1	The EE must be phrased as a question.	☐	☐
2	The criteria have been reduced from 11 to 5 and all are worth equal marks.	☐	☐
3	You are required to complete the RPPF.	☐	☐
4	You are required to complete a Researcher's Reflection Space (RRS).	☐	☐
5	A grade E in the EE is no longer a failing condition.	☐	☐
6	Essays that are descriptive in nature do not score highly.	☐	☐
7	The maximum word limit for the reflection component of the assessment is 500 words.	☐	☐
8	Criterion D (Formal presentation) assesses the structure and layout of your EE.	☐	☐
9	The EE is marked out of a total of 36 points.	☐	☐
10	There is no stipulated limit to the number of hours that a supervisor should spend with a candidate.	☐	☐

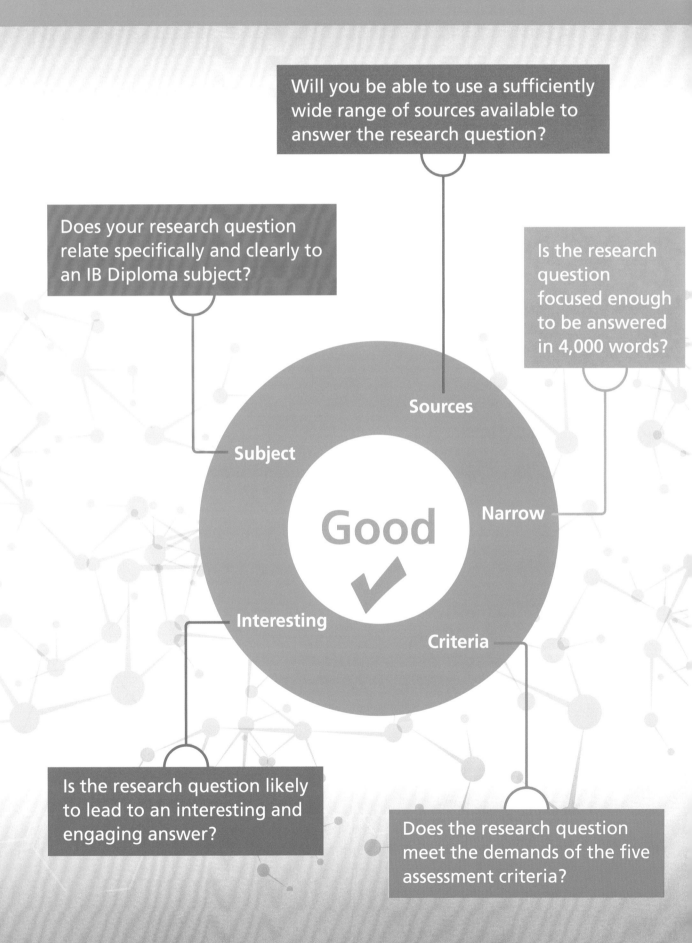

Will you be able to use a sufficiently wide range of sources available to answer the research question?

Does your research question relate specifically and clearly to an IB Diploma subject?

Is the research question focused enough to be answered in 4,000 words?

Sources

Subject

Good ✔

Narrow

Interesting

Criteria

Is the research question likely to lead to an interesting and engaging answer?

Does the research question meet the demands of the five assessment criteria?

suitable titles

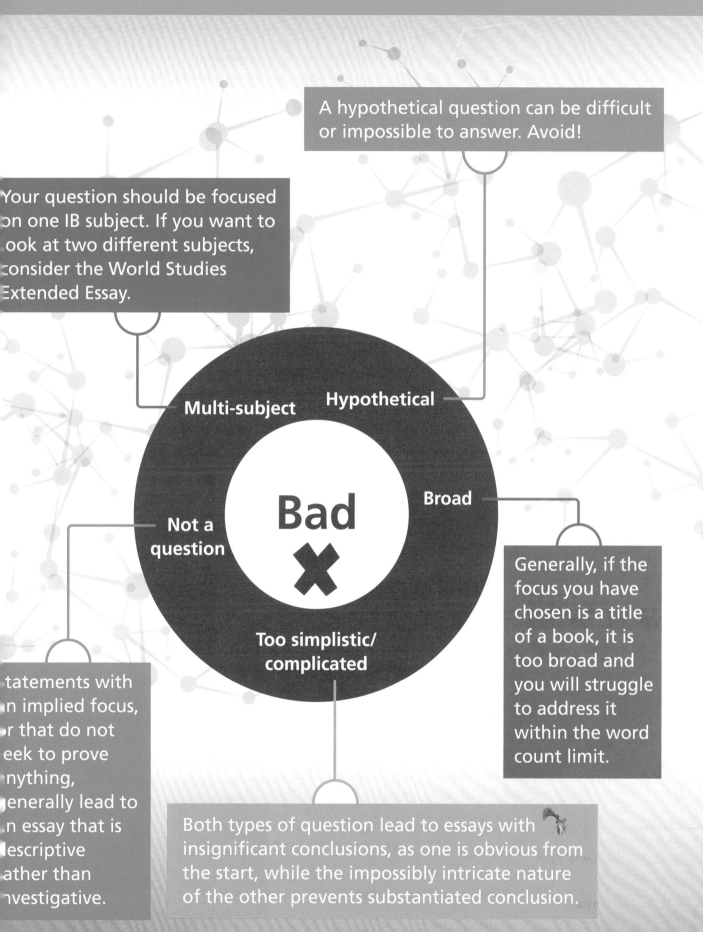

A hypothetical question can be difficult or impossible to answer. Avoid!

Your question should be focused on one IB subject. If you want to look at two different subjects, consider the World Studies Extended Essay.

Multi-subject

Hypothetical

Bad

X

Broad

Not a question

Generally, if the focus you have chosen is a title of a book, it is too broad and you will struggle to address it within the word count limit.

Too simplistic/ complicated

tatements with n implied focus, r that do not eek to prove nything, enerally lead to n essay that is escriptive ather than vestigative.

Both types of question lead to essays with insignificant conclusions, as one is obvious from the start, while the impossibly intricate nature of the other prevents substantiated conclusion.

2 Formulating suitable titles

Choosing a suitable research question

Follow these five steps to developing a good research question:

1 Choose a subject and specific topic that is of genuine interest to you.

2 Make sure you can articulate exactly *why* you are interested in the subject and the specific topic chosen for investigation.

3 Carry out preliminary reading on the chosen topic and then get on with some general reading around the issue.

4 Begin posing open-ended questions about your chosen topic. These questions will usually be framed using the terms 'How', 'Why' or 'To what extent?'

5 Evaluate the research question; make sure your question allows for analysis and the development of a reasoned argument.

Avoid using a research question that is unclear, vague or too broad because you will most probably end up writing a descriptive or narrative essay which will not score well against the assessment criteria. Only a well-phrased research question that creates the opportunity for you to conduct thorough analysis and to present well-reasoned arguments to answer the question will allow examiners to award you the higher mark bands, especially for Criterion C (critical thinking).

Choosing a good research question involves a series of carefully planned steps

Common problems with research questions

■ 1 Too broad

A regular concern expressed in EE reports is the selection of topics that are too broad to be treated effectively within the 4,000-word limit. A simple rule of thumb is that if the focus you have chosen is a title of a book, it is too broad. It would be better to look at the title of the chapters in the book as an indication of a focus more suitable to an EE.

Another way of judging if a topic is too broad is if you are looking at a multiplicity of factors: economic, social and political reasons for something, for example. It would be much better to limit the essay to *one* of these factors for the chosen topic.

If the focus of your research question is too broad, you should be advised to narrow it down. Sometimes the actual intended argument in the essay is not too broad, but you need to make sure that the research question reflects this as well.

> ### EXPERT TIP
> Under the new assessment criteria, students whose research question is too broad self-penalize across all assessment criteria. Make sure you liaise with your supervisor to ensure you have a fit-for-purpose research question.

■ 2 Too simplistic or too complicated

These type of research questions will lead to meaningless outcomes that add little, if any, value to the reader. Titles that are too simplistic are easily accomplished but with an insignificant conclusion as the outcome was probably self-evident and should have been predicted in advance. Titles that are far too complicated do not generate an outcome (or one that has any true purpose or meaning) due to the impossibly intricate nature of the topic.

■ 3 Not a question

Some 'questions' are not phrased as questions – they are merely statements with an implied focus (such as *Wars of German Unification* or *An investigation into the Volkswagen Scandal*) or they do not seek to prove anything. Such titles naturally lead the student to write a purely descriptive account in the essay.

Even questions that are phrased as questions fall into this category. For example, 'What types of currency have existed in Guatemala?' or 'What is inflation? – Zimbabwe as a case study' would lead to a very narrative account and would score badly on Criteria C (critical thinking).

A good research question is not just a question. It should enable you to focus on the analysis and evaluation of the chosen topic, in order for you to generate an original conclusion.

■ Questions about questions

It is important that you ask yourself some good questions about your choice of research question. This will actually help you to determine if your research question is a suitable one for writing the EE.

Questions you should be considering include:

- Is your research question sufficiently narrow? If you're not sure, check with your supervisor.
- What, if anything, has already been written about your chosen topic?
- Will it be realistic for you to find the necessary sources of information for this topic?
- Is there an appropriate range of different sources, views and perspectives available?

There are many questions to consider before settling on a final research question

■ Is the research question specific to a single IB subject? (unless you've chosen to write a World Studies Extended Essay).

■ Will the research question help the reader to understand the value and purpose of your research?

■ Is the research question focused enough to allow you to explore the task within the timeframe and 4,000-word limit?

■ Will your research question provide enough data and information for you to write a sustained argument?

■ Is your research question an interesting one? How do you know?

TASK 1

Copy out the following table and, in the first column, write your three Higher Level subjects. In the column next to these write at least two theses/arguments that you think would be achievable for an EE, but also that challenge preconceived ideas or take a different approach to the norm. Be inventive but realistic!

Higher Level subject	Possible Extended Essay question (phrased as a question) that is unusual, challenging and inventive

COMMON MISTAKE

One way to ensure you avoid losing valuable marks is to ensure your research question is grammatically correct. Too often, students write research questions that are difficult to comprehend and this makes it more challenging for the examiner to understand the scope, direction and purpose of the essay.

EXPERT TIP

Occasionally a student will repeat the structure and expression of a research question from a sample EE that a supervisor might have provided for reference. It is important that you create your own research question in order to encourage a sense of ownership and originality. This is not only vital for academic honesty reasons, but will prove critical during the following months of research. Examiners want you to take the essay seriously at each stage of the process.

The requirement from the IB is that your EE must have a title (that is not phrased as a question) and a research question (phrased as a question).

Possible examples for this are:

■ History EE

'A Hell on earth' (Title)

'To what extent can the Battle of Stalingrad be seen as the most significant turning point of WW2 in Europe?' (Research Question)

■ Economics EE

'Government intervention in the world's freest economy.' (Title)

'To what extent is Hong Kong's Vehicles Registration & Licensing (transport policy) a solution to the problem of traffic congestion?

TASK 2

Suggest a possible research question for these titles:

- 'Charles Dickens – the greatest of all Victorians' (English)
- 'Catch them young – the importance of Drama and Theatre in primary schools' (Theatre)

Suggest a possible title for this research question:

- 'Does John Searle's Chinese Room thought experiment successfully demonstrate that computers cannot think?' (Philosophy)

Now suggest a possible Research question and Title in a subject that you would like to study.

TASK 3

Which of these are good research questions and why? Copy out and complete the table below, then check the answers at the back of this book.

1 A comparison of wars.

2 Aspects of the First World War which led to medical advances.

3 'The fact that she is not immune to *Persuasion* makes Anne Elliot one of Jane Austen's most admirable and sympathetic characters.' Discuss.

4 Can comic books be art?

5 The development of a tragic hero from Homer's *Iliad* to Eddie Carbone in Arthur Miller's *A View from the Bridge*.

6 An investigation and redesign of a rotational laundry rack for elderly people.

7 A comparison of traditional markets and supermarkets.

8 A study of Pi.

9 Do the benefits that Disneyland brings to Paris outweigh the costs?

10 How effective are complex B vitamins in comparison to DEET in preventing mosquito bites?

Essay title number	Good or bad?	Reasons
1		
2		

TASK 4

Choose three of the questions above that are not good questions and re-write them so that they become better questions, suitable for an EE.

TASK 5

What might make a good research question on each of the following topics?

- Adolf Hitler
- Depression
- Population growth
- World's tallest buildings
- Lord of the Rings

A Visual Arts Extended Essay on tall buildings should consider the *aesthetic* aspects of their design

TASK 6

Consider why the following are *not* good research questions. Which subject would they fit into?

- The origins of the Cold War
- English novels
- How to design a space shuttle
- Why should we expect a flu epidemic?
- When should we expect the next tsunami?
- Do Dry Shirts work? How do they work?
- Are Chinese medicines effective?
- Was Albert Einstein an atheist?
- The NBA in China

▨ Formulating a good research question

There are five key areas to consider when determining your research question:

1 **Subject** – does your research question relate specifically and clearly to an IB Diploma subject?

2 **Sources** – will you be able to use a sufficiently wide range of sources available to answer the research question?

3 **Focused** – is the research question narrow enough to be answered in 4,000 words?

4 **Interesting** – is the research question likely to lead to an interesting and engaging answer?

5 **Criteria** – does the research question meet the demands of the five assessment criteria?

Sample research questions (essay titles)

To help you formulate your own research question, this section provides examples of good EE titles from a range of different Diploma Programme subjects.

Group 1	Essay title
English Lang & Lit	How does the superbrand McDonald's maintain its global appeal through advertising techniques?
	To what extent are the changing visual elements and graphology of toy advertisements an indication of changing child gender attitudes since the 1960s?
English Literature	To what extent does the portrayal of transgenderism in Virginia Woolf's 'Orlando; A Biography' serve as a form of empowerment, especially for women?
	How does Thackeray convey the idea that 19th-century English society prioritized external appearance over moral principles in 'Vanity Fair'?

Group 2	Essay title
Spanish	¿Cuál es la importancia de las mujeres en "la casa de Bernarda Alba" y "Bodas de Sangre" por García Lorca?
	What is the importance of women in "The house of Bernarda Alba" and "Blood Wedding" by Garcia Lorca?
	"Agua para Chocolate", ¿Cómo influyen las recetas y los remedios caseros en las interacciones, emociones y amor entre los personajes?
	In the novel "Like Water for Chocolate", how do recipes and home remedies influence the interactions, emotions and love between the characters?

French	Dans quelle mesure les interdictions de fumer dans les lieux publiques sont-elles un avantage pour le reste du monde?
	In what ways can the interdiction to smoke in public places in France be seen as an advantage for the rest of the world?
	Dans quelle mesure peut-on dire que la Loi de 2010 interdisant la dissimulation du visage dans l'espace public en France est-elle une mesure nécessaire pour sauvegarder les valeurs républicaines?
	Is the law of 2010 that prevents covering the face in the public spaces a necessary measure in order to preserve the Republic's values?
Chinese lang A	老北京的成长故事----《城南旧事》中的复调手法体现
	How does the author of novel《my memories of old Beijing》use polyphony to achieve her writing purpose?
	诗歌借鉴的实现方式-----以《繁星春水》为例，探究泰戈尔的《飞鸟集》对冰心诗集风格的影响
	How does the writing style of《Birds Set》written by the poet Tagore influence the Chinese poetry《Flows Stars》written by Chinese poet Bingxin?
Chinese lang B	从香港交通发展的历史看香港社会文化变迁
	How does the change of the traditional Chinese characters to simplified characters affect the learning of Chinese culture?
	浅析繁体字被简体字取代所带来的文化缺失
	How does the development of transportation in Hong Kong represent the culture change of Hong Kong society?
Japanese	日本料理と中国料理
	How is Japanese food different from Chinese food?
	高校生の生活
	In what ways is school life for Japanese high school students and Chinese high school students similar?

Group 3	Essay title
Business management	To what extent has Kellogg's been successful in repositioning its cereal products as health products?
	How effective has McDonald's Create Your Own strategy been in developing market growth?
Economics	To what extent has the fall in the exchange rate of the pound sterling following Brexit affected the tourist industry in the Lake District?
	How will the new minimum wage of Hong Kong affect the stakeholders of Café de Coral?
Geography	To what extent has the environmental levy on plastic bags been successful worldwide? A study based upon two different regions.
	How did the Hong Kong SARS outbreak affect social and economic features of the region?
History	To what extent was the ideology of 'continuous Revolution' the main cause of the Chinese Cultural Revolution?
	To what extent can Lenin's rise to power in 1917 be attributed to foreign intervention?
Philosophy	To what extent has Simone de Beauvoir's existentialism challenged western patriarchal views of female sexuality?
	Can metaphysical interpretations of gender be effectively applied?
Psychology	What factors contribute to females being perceived as attractive?
	To what extent does personality affect relative levels of stress in the medical profession?

Group 4	Essay title
Biology	How does the variation in pigmentation in three different leaves vary the rate at which photosynthesis occurs?
	To what extent does the tar content of different Marlboro brand cigarettes vary when measured by tar content in cotton wool?
Chemistry	How does the increasing number of the methylene group when ascending the alcohol group affect its ability to dissolve fatty acids as a solvent when finding the iodine number?
	To what extent is there a variation in caffeine content in black teas across different brands?
Design Technology	Why is the Mini considered a classic design?
	How can the internal design environment of public housing be used to maximize comfort and safety for residents?
Environmental systems and societies	How do people's attitudes to the environment vary according to income? A case study in the Fo Tan region of Hong Kong.
	What is the ecological value of Jone's Cove at Sai Kung Peninsula and to what extent is it managed sustainably?
Physics	How does the speed of the blades affect the lift of a drone?
	How does the number of layers of padding affect the impact force of a falling mass?
Sports, exercise and health	To what extent does isometric and plyometric training affect the ability to increase driving distance of 16–18 year old male elite golfers?
	Is high intensity interval training or low intensity cardiovascular training more beneficial to teenage fitness?
Information Technology in a Global Society	How has the introduction of mobile technology in smartphones been beneficial to digital business between India and Singapore?
	To what extent can the invasion of privacy caused by modern smartphones be minimized?

Group 5	Essay title
Mathematics	What is the relationship between Poisson and exponential distributions?
	To what extent do musical scales follow a mathematical geometric progression?

Group 6	Essay title
Film	How does John Wells use camera movement, framing and blocking to portray the concept of leadership in the individual in the film 'Burnt'?
	How does lighting contribute effectively to film production?
Music	To what extent is the original flavour of rural Mexican mariachi music retained in its modern urban variant?
	How does Northern classical Indian music impact on modern Western heavy metal musical structure?
Theatre	What are the prominent production values that serve to promote the intentions of Theatre of Comedy and Theatre of the Absurd?
	What are the means by which Drama makes a positive impact on primary years children?
Visual Arts	To what extent is traditional Ukiyo-e printmaking in Japan reflected in contemporary Manga cartoons?
	To what extent has linear perspective become obsolete in contemporary art?

World Studies	How has Angelina Jolie affected perceptions on preventive measures for breast cancer and ovarian cancer?
	Is adopting a vegan diet more ethical and environmentally sustainable than one which contains meat?
	What are the dangers of caesarean section without medical recommendations and why is the rate of C-section in Hong Kong so much higher than the WHO's recommended rate of 15%?

> **EXPERT TIP**
>
> A good research question is the start of good research. Watch this brief YouTube video clip about the difference between a research question and hypothesis: **goo.gl/wKaV6Q**

Understanding the implications

The quality of your research question is relevant to all of the assessment criteria and we'll look now at the impact of your question on the individual criterion.

Criterion A (focus and method) is most clearly related to your choice of a good research question. This criterion focuses on the topic, the research question and the methodology. It considers the extent to which the purpose of your essay is specified and how well you maintain focus (on the research question) throughout.

If the question is not clearly stated or is too broad in scope (given the 4,000-word limit), then your essay will score in the lowest level descriptor (1 to 2 marks). If the research question is more clearly stated but the discussion is only partially focused on your research question, then your essay is likely to score 3 to 4 marks on this criterion. In order to score the top level descriptor on Criterion A (5 to 6 marks), your research question will need to be clearly stated and focused. This enables you to clearly communicate your research and findings in order to connect the discussions in your essay.

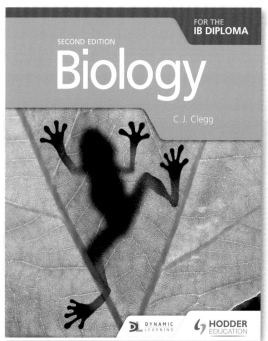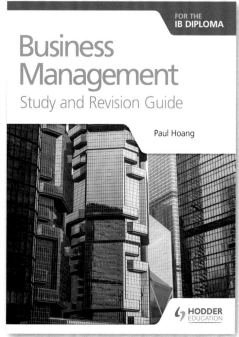

Textbooks and revision guides are good, but you should also look for other sources of information to demonstrate knowledge and understanding

EXPERT TIP

Your research question must be expressed as a question, ending with a question mark.

Criterion B (knowledge and understanding) assesses how effectively you use source materials and subject-specific content in your EE. You will score a low mark (1 to 2 marks) if the evidence used has limited or partial relevance to your research question. Therefore, make sure you choose a research question for which you can find sufficient and good supporting evidence. If you cannot gather the necessary information from a variety of sources, it may be better to simply switch to a different research question. However, do not rely on only textbooks and/or the internet.

EXPERT TIP

Students often wonder what is an appropriate number of sources to use in their essay. The answer to this varies tremendously depending upon the topic selected for research. There are some very good essays which have relatively few sources because of the nature of the topic studied. In general, make sure all of your sources help to directly address the research question. Check with your supervisor if you are unsure.

Criterion C (critical thinking) is worth the highest number of marks (12 marks). It assesses your critical thinking skills in relation to your research, analysis and discussion (evaluation), which must be directly relevant to the research question. If these are only partially relevant, you can expect to score no more than 6 marks for Criterion C. For the top level descriptor (10 to 12 marks) you will need to demonstrate that research, analysis and discussion are *consistently* relevant to your research question. Hence, having a clearly defined and focused research question is vital to score well on Criterion C.

For **Criterion D (formal presentation)**, worth up to 4 marks, you will need to show that the structure and layout of your EE supports the reading, understanding and evaluation of the topic stated in your research question. A good research question is a vital part of this structure and underpins the quality of your methodology, analysis, understanding and discussion of the essay. A poor choice of research question is likely to undermine everything you are trying to achieve.

Finally, for **Criterion E (engagement)**, worth up to 6 marks, your supervisor will be looking for evidence of engagement right from the start of the writing process. Hence, choosing an interesting research question will improve the chances of scoring well on this criterion (which is based on your level of engagement as shown in your Reflections on Planning and Progress Form). Having a good research question helps you to show a high degree of intellectual and personal engagement with the work and a willingness to be academically creative, imaginative and original. The choice of research question is the first step in this – choose a question carefully that is authentic and original and that genuinely inspires your interest. This also ensures your essay is interesting and shows your true engagement.

CHAPTER SUMMARY KEY POINTS

- Avoid using a research question that is unclear, vague or too broad.

- Do not make your question too simplistic or too complicated.

- Choose a research question on a subject that is of genuine interest to you.

- Your research question must be phrased as a question.

- Your research question should lend itself to a good range of accessible and relevant sources.

- A good research question is vital to scoring well on all of the assessment criteria, especially Criterion A (focus and method).

- The best EEs consider carefully how the research question relates to all of the assessment criteria.

■ END OF CHAPTER QUIZ

	Question	True	False
1	The research question should always be phrased as a question.	☐	☐
2	Criterion A (focus and method) is concerned specifically with the quality of the research question.	☐	☐
3	Criterion A (focus and method) is worth 12 marks.	☐	☐
4	The research question may fall into a number of subject areas as long as those subjects are clearly stated.	☐	☐
5	A descriptive research question is likely to lead to a narrative essay which will score poorly on Criterion C (critical thinking).	☐	☐
6	A World Studies Extended Essay research question may focus on any number of IB subjects.	☐	☐
7	It is permitted to change or alter your EE research question even after starting research and meeting with your supervisor.	☐	☐
8	The research question has no direct relevance to Criterion D (presentation).	☐	☐
9	Your research question should be restated in the introduction of your EE.	☐	☐
10	The research question should be very specific and narrow to allow for effective treatment within the essay word limit of 4,000 words.	☐	☐

The formal presentation

Title page

Contents page

1.
2.
3.
4.
5.
6.
7.

Essay Title

Introduction

Body
(development/methods/results)

Footnotes
(if used)

WORD COUNT
(4,000 words)

Body
(development/methods/results)

Conclusion

Endnotes
(if used)

Bibliography

Appendices

3

The formal presentation of the Extended Essay

The formal presentation of the Extended Essay (EE)

The EE should be presented in the following format:

- Title page
- Contents page
- Introduction
- Body (development/methods/results)
- Conclusion
- References and bibliography
- Appendices – this is not a formal requirement, but if used must be placed after the references and bibliography.

As the EE must be anonymized, it is vital that you do not include your candidate name or number anywhere in your EE, be it the title page or within the essay (such as in a header or footer). The name of your school or the centre number should not be included either.

You must adhere to the required formatting of the EE. It is highly recommended that you use the following format:

- Arial font
- Size 12 font
- Double line spacing
- Portrait orientation (landscape is acceptable only for graphs or illustrations where required)
- A4 size
- Numbered pages.

Producing the essay in this format also helps examiners. Not only does it make the presentation more consistent than before, it also facilitates on-screen assessment of the essay.

Whilst an academic paper, such as the EE, should include items in the appendices, these must be used carefully and purposefully. Examiners are not required to check or read anything included in the appendices, so anything that you want read should be included in the essay itself. Only supplementary evidence should be included in the appendix, but this should be selected with care and kept to a minimum. For example, students writing a World Studies Extended Essay should include their Researcher's Reflection Space (RRS) – looked at in more detail in Chapter 7. Essentially, the examiner should be able to read and understand your essay without having to access external web links or accompanying source materials, such as documentaries or news media articles. Remember, examiners are not required to refer to any material that is not included in the essay itself.

EXPERT TIP

An abstract is no longer a formal requirement for the EE.

Your essay must be presented in an orderly manner

The Extended Essay is an academic piece of work that should be produced using a computer, wherever possible

Candidates must declare their word count on the title page of the EE. As you need to upload an electronic version of your EE, it becomes very easy for the examiner to determine where the essay has reached 4,000 words (the word limit). The IB allows students to use footnotes for referencing purposes only, so anyone trying to use footnotes to bypass the word count will simply be penalized. It also helps to ensure greater parity across different subjects.

The EE is a written (or typed) piece of academic work. This may include the use of accompanying still images, photos, diagrams and charts. However, there is no provision made for the inclusion of any other digital media, such as audio or visual attachments.

COMMON MISTAKE

Too often, students will use their Internal Assessment work and lengthen this to write their EE. There are two issues here: candidates cannot 'double dip' as this is considered to be academic malpractice. In addition, the assessment criteria for the EE differ from the IA.

■ Research question

Your research question must be phrased as a question. This will help you to maintain focus more easily when writing the EE. The research question must appear on the front title page of your essay. The purpose and the focus of your research must be clear and appropriate.

The IB uploads exemplar EEs, with examiner marks and comments, to the Programme Resource Centre (PRC). Make sure you speak with your supervisor about getting access to these exemplars so you can see how the EE should be formally presented. It will also allow you to see examples of good research questions.

EXPERT TIP

Before you embark on writing the essay, be sure that you can access a range of relevant sources and apply subject-specific theories, tools and techniques to the research question.

■ Diagrams, photos and illustrations

It is important to pay attention to the presentation and overall neatness of your essay. This includes any illustrative materials that you use, such as diagrams, maps, tables, charts, graphs and illustrations. These must be fully and clearly labelled so they can be easily interpreted by the examiner. The labels used for these must not include a commentary, as this will be considered as part of the word count. Of course, the explanations should be included as part of the essay so that the examiner can understand the relevance and significance of these.

Do not try to circumvent the word count by including analysis, discussion or evaluation in data tables

EXPERT TIP

Whilst the use of photos and other images is acceptable, you should avoid the excessive use of these as they may detract from the discussion in your EE. If and where used, these must be relevant to the point of discussion being made.

■ Tables

It is acceptable to include tables to show data and/or information related to the research question. However, these should be used carefully as they are only appropriate in certain subjects, such as Economics or Geography. Tables must never be used in an attempt to exceed the 4,000-word limit as this will get detected.

■ Footnotes and endnotes

Footnotes and endnotes, if used in the EE, must only be used for referencing purposes. Any text in a footnote or endnote that is not used for referencing will be included in the word count by the examiner. Nevertheless, it is worth noting that footnotes and endnotes are *not* required in the EE. For example, students may prefer to reference using the Modern Languages Association (MLA) style, which uses in-text citation instead (see Chapter 5).

Make sure that all information that is of direct relevance to the discussion of the research question is included within the body of the essay. Including such information in the footnotes or endnotes (or even the appendices) will simply be included in the word count by the examiner.

EXPERT TIP

Prevention is better than cure – rather than risk losing marks by exceeding the word limit, even if unintentional, you should avoid using footnotes or endnotes unless these are for referencing purposes.

■ Citations of the Extended Essay

Citations are used to make references within the body of the EE, usually as in-text citations or as footnotes/endnotes. Hence, this is produced in short form, rather than in its entirety. A citation must provide the examiner with an accurate reference so that s/he can easily locate the source. Hence, citations should normally include the page number(s) when referencing printed materials, such as textbooks, academic journals or novels. This must be the case when using direct quotations from printed publications.

EXPERT TIP

When using citations, the full reference must still be included. However, these are recorded at the end of the essay in the bibliography.

How you cite the various sources used in your EE will depend on the particular referencing style that you have chosen (see Chapter 5 for further details). The important thing, from the IB's perspective, is the format of citations must be consistently produced and presented.

■ Referencing of the Extended Essay

A reference is used to acknowledge and indicate information was obtained from a source other than the author. It enables the reader to verify knowledge claims and the information or data that has been presented in the EE. References can come from a variety of sources, such as textbooks, trade magazines, academic journals, newspapers, interviews and internet websites.

The IB does not prescribe a specific style of referencing. However, your EE supervisor and/or school Librarian should be able to help you with this. It would be useful if the school had a uniform referencing style, be it the MLA, APA, Harvard, Chicago or other recognized style. Whichever style is used, it must be applied consistently throughout the essay and enable the examiner to trace the source.

See Chapter 5 for more specific details and guidance about proper citation and referencing in the EE.

EXPERT TIP

It is highly recommended that you properly reference your sources from the outset. Make sure you include references (and citations, if used) in your first draft. This will reduce any suspicion of plagiarism and also save you a huge amount of work on submission of the final draft.

COMMON MISTAKE

Too often, students include the URL of the websites they have used but do not include the full reference in the bibliography. It is even worse when a generic website is cited or 'referenced', such as **http://www.bbc.co.uk/news/business**.

■ Bibliography

A bibliography contains the list of all sources used in researching and writing the EE. This should include any sources that have not been cited in the body of the essay but were used to inform the writing of the EE. It is acceptable to place such sources in the acknowledgment. In all cases, the bibliography must list all those sources cited in the essay. This should be produced in alphabetical order.

EXPERT TIP

Make use of the many online resources to help you to produce the bibliography. For example, EasyBib (**http://www.easybib.com/**) is a free bibliography generator for all major referencing formats, such as MLA, APA, Chicago and Harvard. There is clear advice on how to include websites, books, videos, films, journals and databases in your bibliography.

Your bibliography must list all sources used in your research

> **EXPERT TIP**
>
> Only your written essay is assessed. There is no need to include audio and/or digital resources, as these are not considered to be part of the EE submission (apart from acknowledging them in your bibliography). Hence, do not include audio or digital resources when submitting and uploading your essay.

■ Appendices

Appendices are not a necessary component of the EE. Although they tend to be used to provide supplementary evidence of the research conducted, examiners are not expected or required to read the information in the appendices.

Therefore, if you choose to include items in the appendices, make sure the materials have direct relevance to your analysis, arguments and conclusion. The following are examples of what is acceptable to include in the appendices:

■ Copy of a completed questionnaire used as primary research in the essay

■ Transcript of interview questions and answers used as part of the research in the essay

■ Copy of any permission letters to carry out research for academic purposes

■ Copies of poems or short stories (of less than three pages) for EEs in Group 1, category 1 and in language acquisition, category 3

■ Excerpts from newspapers, advertisements and transcripts of speeches for EEs in Group 1, category 3 and in language acquisition, category 1 and 2

■ Raw data or statistical tables for EEs in experimental sciences.

In all the above cases, there should not be any analysis, discussion or conclusions included in the appendices.

Although citation and referencing are an integral aspect of academic writing, you should avoid continually referring to the materials in the appendices. Examiners are not expected to refer to the materials there and it could disrupt the flow of the essay as they read and mark your work.

■ Word limit

The IB enforces a very strict rule on the 4,000 words allowed for an EE – examiners are instructed not to read any material in excess of the word limit. However, the 4,000-word limit does not include the following:

■ Acknowledgements*

■ Contents page

■ Maps

■ Charts

■ Diagrams

■ Annotated illustrations

■ Tables

■ Equations, formulae and calculations

■ References (footnotes or end notes)

Do not exceed the word limit

- Bibliography
- Appendices.

* Note: due to the requirement to anonymize the Extended Essay, you must not acknowledge your teacher by name or any other member of your school community.

It is vital therefore that your research question must be sufficiently focused to allow you to manage and complete the EE within the word limit.

> **COMMON MISTAKE**
>
> A common mishap is that candidates do not check the accuracy of the page numbers in their contents page. This can leave a bad impression on the examiner.

> **EXPERT TIP**
>
> If you have exceeded your word limit before final submission, proofread the essay and edit this to no more than 4,000 words. To help, check that all aspects of your essay relate specifically to the research question.

■ The Reflections on Planning and Progress Form

Finally, it is important to remember that all EEs must be submitted (uploaded) with the Reflections on Planning and Progress Form (RPPF). This is a mandatory requirement for all essays, and is formally assessed under Criterion E. See Chapter 7 for more details about reflections and the RPPF and how to complete the form.

You should also look at the advice provided by the IB here: **https://goo.gl/mkcJ4n** (a PowerPoint presentation produced and delivered by Angela Rivière in her position as Curriculum Manager for the EE).

The electronic upload of the Extended Essay

Since November 2016, schools have been required to upload all EEs. Schools do not have an option to send hard copies of the EE to examiners. This has meant that the formal presentation of the EE has become ever more important.

There are a number of ways that schools can upload the EE:

1 The EE supervisor uploads and verifies the authenticity of the candidate's essay, thereby formally submitting it for external assessment.

2 The IB Diploma Programme Coordinator does the above.

3 The candidate uploads his or her own essay – but this still requires the EE supervisor or IB Diploma Programme Coordinator to verify the authenticity of the candidate's essay.

The vast majority of EEs are produced using computer software, such as Microsoft Word, Pages and Google Docs. The IB allows students to submit handwritten EEs, but these need to be scanned and uploaded in the same way as those produced on a computer. In some subjects, such as Economics, hand-drawn diagrams are often produced, but again these must be scanned for electronic upload.

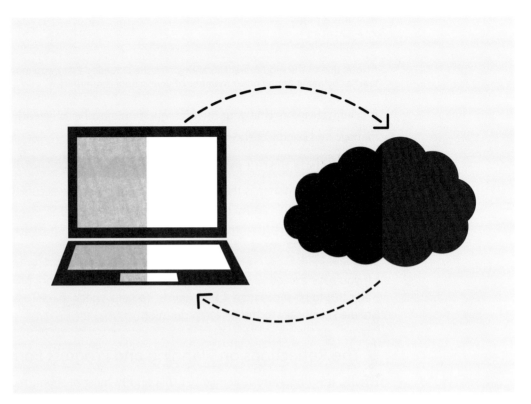

All Extended Essays must be electronically uploaded for assessment

Your EE must be saved in an acceptable file format. The IB recommends any one of the following file types:

- **.doc** – Microsoft Word document
- **.docx** – the newer version of Microsoft Word (the format is not backward compatible)
- **.pdf** – Adobe Acrobat's portable document format
- **.rtf** – Microsoft's rich text format that is readable on most word-processing software.

Whilst the EE should be saved using one of the above formats, the overall size of the file must not exceed 10 megabytes (MB). This should still be sufficient for the inclusion of any high-quality photos, diagrams or images that you wish to include in the essay.

> **EXPERT TIP**
>
> Scanning hand-drawn images (such as diagrams, tables, maps and charts) will tend to increase the file size of your EE. Where possible, always try to produce these in digital format.

The exact instructions for the electronic uploading of the EE is outlined in the *Diploma Programme Assessment Procedures* and on IBIS for IB Coordinators. Be sure to check with your supervisor so you are confident about the procedures for uploading your EE. The process is very similar to that of the electronic uploading of your Theory of Knowledge essays.

CHAPTER SUMMARY KEY POINTS

- The EE should be presented in the following format:
  - Title page
  - Contents page
  - Introduction
  - Body (development/methods/results)
  - Conclusion
  - References and bibliography
  - Appendices.
- The essay should be formatted as follows:
  - Arial font
  - Size 12 font
  - Double spacing
  - Numbered pages.
- Do not include an abstract; it is no longer required.
- The essay must be anonymized throughout, so there mustn't be anything that enables the examiner to identify the candidate by name or by their school.
- Footnotes/endnotes can be used, but only for referencing purposes.
- References must be used in the essay (in-text citations can also be used).
- Handwritten EEs or those that include hand-drawn illustrations/diagrams must be scanned for upload.
- Electronically uploaded files must not exceed 10MB.

EXPERT TIP

Take a look at the checklist on pages 111–113 for further guidance on the formal presentation of the EE.

■ END OF CHAPTER QUIZ

	Question	True	False
1	The title page must include the research question.	☐	☐
2	A contents page must be included, with page numbering.	☐	☐
3	Examiners are required to access external sources or supplementary information in the appendices.	☐	☐
4	Hand-drawn diagrams or illustrations must be scanned for electronic upload.	☐	☐
5	Any information contained in a footnote or endnote will not be included in the word count.	☐	☐
6	The IB highly recommends candidates to use Arial font, in font size 12, to present the EE.	☐	☐
7	The IB requires candidates to use the Modern Languages Association (MLA) referencing system in the EE.	☐	☐
8	Appendices are not a necessary component of the EE.	☐	☐
9	You need to use your candidate number to upload the EE.	☐	☐
10	Reflections are formally assessed in the EE.	☐	☐

Academic honesty

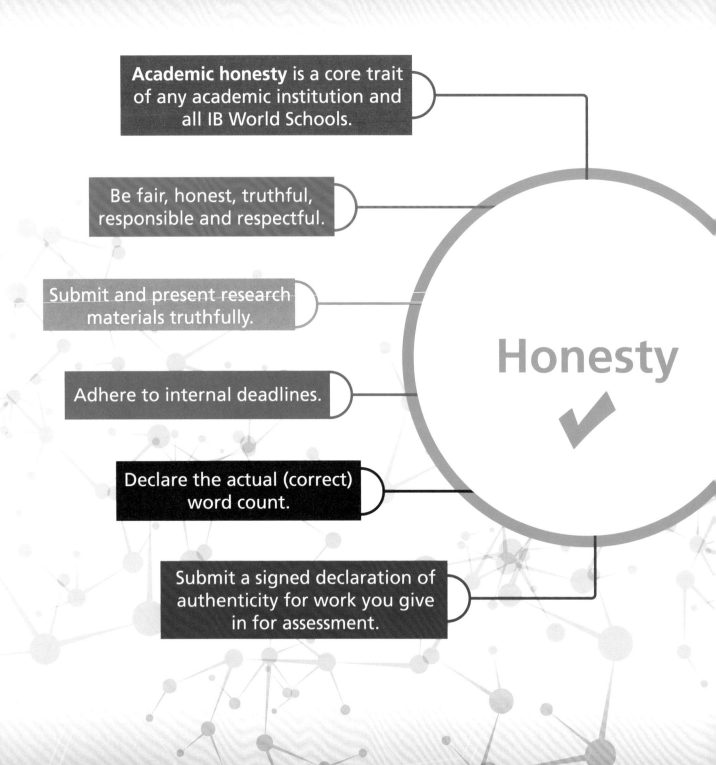

Academic honesty is a core trait of any academic institution and all IB World Schools.

Be fair, honest, truthful, responsible and respectful.

Submit and present research materials truthfully.

Adhere to internal deadlines.

Declare the actual (correct) word count.

Submit a signed declaration of authenticity for work you give in for assessment.

Honesty ✔

Plagiarism – pretending the words, ideas or opinions of another person are your own.

Collusion – supporting the academic dishonesty of another student, for example, allowing a friend to copy your work.

Fabrication of research data – making up your results.

Duplication of work – submitting parts of, or all of, one piece of work for multiple different components of assessment – this is sometimes known as 'double dipping'.

Dishonesty

Gaining an unfair advantage – any act that gives you unfair advantage, for example, missing deadlines, under-declaring the word count, getting someone else to write your essay.

4 Academic honesty and the Extended Essay

What is academic honesty?

Academic honesty is a code of conduct based on approaching your academic studies in an honest, truthful, responsible, fair and respectful manner. It is a philosophy about valuing intellectual property rights. It is a core trait of any academic institution and all IB World Schools. By contrast, academic dishonesty refers to any action that results in a student gaining an unfair advantage for a piece of assessed work, such as the Extended Essay (EE) or an Internal assessment.

Examples of academic dishonesty include:

- **Plagiarism** – A student presents the words, ideas or opinions of another person as though it was their own. This act also infringes the copyrights of others.

- **Collusion** – This refers to the act of one student supporting the academic dishonesty of another student. For example, a student might choose to allow a friend to copy his or her ideas or work for formal assessment purposes.

- **Fabrication of research data** – Fabricating and presenting research data as though they were authentic in an Internal Assessment or the EE is academic malpractice. This might include, for example, falsifying primary research data, such as interviews or questionnaires.

- **Duplication of work** – Also called 'double dipping', this refers to the presentation and submission of the same work (in part or in entirety) for different components of internal and/or external assessment. For example, students who submit their EE using part of their work from an Internal Assessment would be regarded as academically dishonest.

- **Gaining an unfair advantage** – Any act that enables a candidate to gain an unfair advantage is considered academic dishonesty. Examples of such academic malpractice include:

  □ Fabricating the use of secondary research, such as textbooks or academic journals that have been referred to in the EE

  □ Missing the internal deadline for submitting the first (and only) draft of the EE

  □ Using a commercial service provider or any third party to write the EE on behalf of the student

  □ Dishonesty by under-declaring the word count of the EE.

솔직한

onestà

honestidad

honnêteté

honesty

诚信为本

Academic honesty is a core principle in IB World Schools

> **EXPERT TIP**
>
> Academic honesty applies to all assessment work, not just the EE. Make sure you comply with the same standards and practices for your IAs, IOCs, written assignments, TOK essays and final IB examinations.

> **EXPERT TIP**
>
> A growing number of cases of malpractice are reported by 'whistle blowers', often via IB Answers (**https://ibanswers.ibo.org/**). These include parents (who are disgruntled about the academic malpractice of other students) and teachers (from other schools!). All schools are profiled and all cases of suspected malpractice are logged by the IBO.

■ What is plagiarism?

Plagiarism is often interpreted as copying the work of others, usually without citing the source. Whilst this is indeed plagiarism, there is more to it. Understanding the meaning and academic interpretation of plagiarism is fundamental to effective prevention of academic malpractice. Other examples of such malpractice include:

- Submitting the work of another person as your own. For example, this could be the work of another candidate or that written by someone for commercial purposes.

- Work which contains text that has been copied and pasted from a source without any alterations and/or proper citation.

- Re-arranging or re-phrasing the words of an author without citing the source. Paraphrasing is still plagiarism if the source is not credited.

- Using another person's ideas, words or examples without using any citation.

- Using someone else's image or photo without stating the source. By default, if you use a photo or image without crediting the source, you are claiming the photo or image to be your own work.

- Submitting the same assessment work for two different components of your Diploma. For example, a Business Management student cannot submit an Internal Assessment on the promotional strategy of Nike and use this same paper for his or her EE about the effectiveness of Nike's advertising strategies.

- Fabricating sources, that is, citing sources that don't actually exist.

EXPERT TIP

If your EE contains images, diagrams or photos from the internet, make sure you specify the exact URL so that the source can be traced. Do not use generic website addresses, such as **www.google.com** or **https://pixabay.com/**

In many schools, formal assessments (such as Internal Assessments, EEs and written assignments) are submitted to plagiarism-detection software, such as Turnitin. A high text match may warrant further investigation by the school and IB Diploma Programme Coordinator.

Copying the work of others is academically dishonest

What are the IBO rules?

The IBO requires EE candidates to have a signed declaration of authenticity for the work submitted for assessment. The IBO reserves the right to ask for proof of candidate authentication. An example of such a declaration is shown below:

> I confirm that this work is my own work and is the final version. I have acknowledged each use of the words or ideas of another person, whether written or oral.
>
> **Signed** ………………………
>
> **Date** ………………………………

Source: Adapted from IBDP *Coordinator's notes*, February 2016

Academic honesty requires students to meet **internal deadlines** set by the school. This means that no student can gain an unfair advantage by missing the school's deadlines. If you need to request an extension for the internal deadline, this must be administered by your school's IB Diploma Coordinator along with all necessary supporting documents.

Please note that all EEs are checked by the IBO using text-matching software for possible collusion and plagiarism. The use of online tools, such as Turnitin can help students and teachers to identify potential problems before a final draft is handed in. More sophisticated software, such as Cactus 64 allows the IBO to check for potential malpractice between candidates submitting work for assessment, such as the Extended Essay.

Any potential breach of the rules and regulations will be investigated by the IBO. This could result in the candidate not receiving a grade for the subject. In the worst-case scenario, the IBO will disqualify the candidate for proven plagiarism, collusion, double dipping or any other type of academic dishonesty. Retaking the IB Diploma qualification is then at the discretion of the IBO.

EXPERT TIP

In the case of suspected academic malpractice, the IBO may request a full written report from your school. The IBO will then take up the case, with the Final Award Committee making a decision whether to disqualify the candidate. Your school's university reference may not be able to guarantee the student's integrity.

Word limits and academic honesty

There are clear expectations about word limits for all work submitted for assessment. The 4,000-word limit for all EEs is no different. Examiners are instructed to not read any part of the essay that is beyond the word limit.

Therefore, candidates who submit their essay in excess of 4,000 words will self-penalize themselves on all five assessment criteria. For example, if the candidate's conclusions appear after the 4,000th word, s/he would lose marks under Criterion C (critical thinking) and Criterion D (formal presentation). Any knowledge and understanding (Criterion B) shown in the essay after the 4,000th word is simply disregarded.

Included in the 4,000 word count	Not included in the 4,000 word count
The introduction	The contents page
The main body of the essay	Maps, charts, diagrams, annotated illustrations
The conclusion	Data tables
Quotations	Equations, formulae and calculations
Footnotes not used for referencing	Citations and references
Endnotes not used for referencing	The bibliography
	The appendices
	The Reflections on Planning and Progress Form

Source: Adapted from IBDP *Extended Essay Guide*, page 85

Finally, please note there is no level of tolerance for the word limit – otherwise it wouldn't be a word limit. Examiners are instructed not to read beyond the 4,000th word. The excessive or inappropriate use of footnotes or endnotes is also frowned upon. Too often, students use footnotes in an attempt to circumvent the word count; doing so is considered to be academic malpractice.

> **EXPERT TIP**
>
> As all EEs are electronically uploaded, this makes it very simple for examiners and moderators to identify where the 4,000-word limit has been reached. This becomes the cut-off point for formal assessment of the EE.

CASE STUDY: CANDIDATE WW, SCHOOL S

WW attended School S, a high-achieving IB World School. However, he was awarded a zero mark in his Geography Higher Level Internal Assessment component by the IBO's Final Award Committee after they concluded that he had plagiarized his coursework. This was a major contributing factor to WW gaining fewer than 12 points in his Higher Level subjects. Unfortunately, this is one of the nine failing conditions, so WW was unsuccessful in gaining the IB Diploma.

Put another way, academic dishonesty can most certainly jeopardize your IB Diploma. It can also bring the reputation of your school to disrepute. Violating the principles of academic honesty can certainly threaten the integrity and reputation of your school as a centre of academic excellence.

Deadlines and academic honesty

As an IB World School, your school or college should have a deadlines policy and have this clearly communicated to teachers, students and parents. A school deadlines policy is an integral element of academic honesty.

A candidate cannot gain an advantage by missing official school/internal deadlines. If the assessment work is submitted after an internal deadline, the supervisor might not be able to authenticate the work to be entirely the student's own. In cases of suspected academic dishonesty, the essay might need to be submitted to the IBO as an atypical piece of work.

Do note that the IB rules state (in the *Diploma Programme Assessment Procedures*) short-term illness is not a valid reason for submitting an incomplete piece of work for assessment (other than for missing an actual IB examination). This is because the assessment, such as the EE, will have been done over a certain length of time, with sufficient time for the candidate to complete the work. The EE, for example, is done over a 40-hour period, with 3 to 5 hours of supervision including time for the three mandatory reflection sessions. This means there is plenty of scope and opportunity for candidates to complete their essay.

The *Diploma Programme Assessment Procedures* clearly states that situations deemed to be reasonably within the control of a candidate would be unacceptable as reasons for submitting incomplete assessment work. These manageable situations include missing the EE deadline due to:

- Misreading and/or misunderstanding the deadline for final submission of the EE
- Oversleeping and therefore being late in submitting the essay
- A family holiday (vacation)
- Moving house
- Participation in a social engagement, such as a graduation ceremony
- Participation in a competition, concert, field trip or sporting event
- Attendance at an interview.

Source: Adapted from the IB *Diploma Programme Assessment Procedures* – Candidates with incomplete work for assessment

Ultimately, the IB Assessment Centre relies on the professional judgement of your teachers.

The first submission of an Internal Assessment, written assignment, TOK essay or EE must be a complete draft. This is important for academic honesty reasons as a complete submission enables your EE supervisor to provide written feedback in a holistic way. It also makes it easier to authenticate the final version of the completed essay.

In special circumstances that are beyond your control, such as a serious family or medical emergency, you should contact the school's IB Diploma Programme Coordinator to request an extension of the deadline. The Coordinator must submit the application with the necessary supporting documents, such as medical certificates, a certified doctor's note or a hospital admission letter. If the request for an extension is authorized by the IB Assessment Centre, this decision will be formally communicated to your school's IB Coordinator via email.

EXPERT TIP

If you become ill around the time of an internal (school) deadline for the submission of any formal assessment work (such as the EE, IOC, TOK essay or an IA), you must contact your school's IB Diploma Programme Coordinator for advice.

■ Responsibilities of teachers (supervisors)

Academic honesty is integral to a school's values and the IB Learner Profile of being principled. As such, all staff and students have an obligation to follow the guidelines set in your school's academic honesty policy. For example, teachers should be aware that only one draft of the EE is allowed. Drafting and redrafting of the EE is deemed to be in breach of academic honesty as this gives candidates an unfair advantage.

Academic honesty should be integral to all aspects of feedback, marking and moderation of assessed work. Supervisors must ensure the fair and transparent treatment of all deadlines so that everyone is consistent in their approach to academic honesty and deadlines.

Oversleeping is not an acceptable reason for missing an internal deadline

Teachers are likely to communicate with parents if there are any concerns about a particular student's academic honesty, such as suspected cases of malpractice, missed deadlines or incomplete work. They should also notify the IB Diploma Programme Coordinator in such cases.

> **EXPERT TIP**
>
> Supervisors must not edit any part of your essay to correct spelling, punctuation or grammar. They must not annotate your essay in such a way that it changes the content of your work.

Refer to Chapter 6 for more details about the role and responsibilities of the EE supervisor.

Responsibilities of students

In completing your EE (or any assessment work), it is important that you:

- Submit and present research materials truthfully
- Cite and reference your work appropriately (see section below)
- Adhere to internal deadlines set by your school
- Submit a complete draft, as written feedback cannot be provided if you miss a deadline
- Declare the actual (correct) word count
- Attend all three reflection sessions with your supervisor
- Sign the declaration of authenticity.

Whilst collaboration is an important way of learning for many people, you must understand the difference between collusion and collaboration. During the collaborative process, you share ideas. Collusion would be academic malpractice as the work you are preparing or presenting is not wholly your own. Instead, you should focus on preparing, writing and presenting your individual and personal essay. Any ideas of other people, be they collaborators or scholars, should always be referred to (see below for section on citation and referencing).

Avoid academic dishonesty in the hope that you won't get caught

> **EXPERT TIP**
>
> Be sure to proofread your research findings to avoid suspicions of malpractice. For example, consider the following statement from a real candidate: *"35% of the [25 people] sample said that they preferred…"*. Whilst this might have been unintentional, many examiners would question the integrity of the research conducted.

> **EXPERT TIP**
>
> Being academically honest will require you to:
>
> ■ Communicate regularly with your EE supervisor
>
> ■ Avoid using EE titles from previous years
>
> ■ Ask for any necessary help from your EE supervisor, EE Coordinator and Librarian
>
> ■ Submit a complete first draft EE of up to 4,000 words
>
> ■ Meet the final submission deadline.

Citation and referencing

The EE is an academic piece of work, so it is expected that you cite all your sources. By using proper citation and referencing, you are showing the EE examiner how you derived your main findings and conclusions. This also includes acknowledging the work of other people in order for you to draw the conclusion to your EE title question. Referencing is vital in enabling the examiner to have the necessary information to locate the source of your information, such as a particular academic journal you used or the person who you interviewed as part of your academic research.

You must provide a citation when:

- Referring to a source
- Stating the words, opinions, ideas or research of someone else
- Using a photo or image created by another person.

It is not necessary to provide a citation when you are expressing:

- Your own opinions or ideas about a particular issue, subject or event
- Common knowledge, such as Paris being the capital city of France.

Even if proper citation and referencing are used, this may still be considered as academic malpractice if the EE over-relies on the work of someone else and lacks originality.

Although there aren't any marks explicitly awarded for citation and referencing in the EE, all students are expected to do so for reasons of academic honesty. Incorrect referencing is viewed as academic dishonesty so can actually result in a fail. Remember, failing the EE is one of the nine failing conditions in the IB Diploma.

EXPERT TIP

To avoid any potential issues with academic malpractice, when in doubt about whether you need to cite something, simply just do it!

IB LEARNER PROFILE

Being academically honest is aligned with being **principled** – do the right thing, even when no one else is watching you.

■ Guidance on educating for academic honesty

Your school, being an IB World School, is expected to approach education about academic honesty in line with the IBO's expectations. For example, ask your school about the guidelines for proper citation and referencing (C&R). Some schools prescribe a particular C&R referencing system, be it the MLA, Chicago, APA or other system.

IB students and EE supervisors are advised to refer to the following two IB publications for further guidance on academic honesty:

- Academic Honesty in the IB educational context (**goo.gl/45wFDI**)
- Effective citing and referencing (**goo.gl/YqvYc5**).

You can also read the presentation from Dr Celina Garza, the IB's Academic Honesty Manager in Cardiff. The presentation was used at the IB Regional Conference in Rome, in late 2014:
goo.gl/YsR4ON.

If you prefer, watch this 10-minute YouTube video from the IB about academic honesty:
goo.gl/rv57iv.

Finally, you are advised to read the article 'Citation and Referencing' by John Royce featured in *IB Review*, April 2016, published by Hodder Education. John Royce is a leading expert on academic honesty and co-author of the IB publication *Effective citing and referencing*.

IB review, April 2016

EXPERT TIP

Supervisors and students should note that 100% of assessment work received by the IBO, including the EE, is checked via sophisticated text-matching software for possible collusion and plagiarism. Any work beyond the word limit for an IA, EE or written assignment is simply not read by examiners.

CHAPTER SUMMARY KEY POINTS

- Academic honesty requires you to plan, write and submit your EE in a fair, honest, truthful, responsible and respectful manner.

- You must provide a signed declaration of authenticity for your work, stating the final version of the essay is your original work.

- Only one complete draft of the EE is allowed to be looked at by your supervisor.

- In suspected cases of academic malpractice, the school is required to conduct an investigation and the IB Diploma Programme Coordinator must provide a written report to the IBO with relevant documentation concerning the case.

- In the worst-case scenario, a candidate may be withdrawn from the IB Diploma Programme on the grounds of academic malpractice.

- Academic honesty is a core trait of any academic institution and all IB World Schools.

	Question	True	False
	■ END OF CHAPTER QUIZ		
1	Academic honesty is a code of conduct based on the principles of trust, honesty, responsibility, fairness and respect.	■	■
2	Allowing a friend to use parts of your own work is considered as collaboration so is not deemed to be academic malpractice.	■	■
3	Plagiarism is an example of academic dishonesty.	■	■
4	It is not necessary to state the exact URL for an image, photo or diagram downloaded from Google.	■	■
5	It is acceptable to use aspects of your market research in an Internal Assessment for your EE.	■	■
6	You must cite and reference your work appropriately.	■	■
7	Schools are expected to use anti-plagiarism software to detect academic malpractice.	■	■
8	Copying the work of others is academically dishonest.	■	■
9	Academic honesty requires you to meet all internal deadlines set by the school.	■	■
10	Competing in a sporting event or school competition exempts you from submitting your essay by the official school deadline.	■	■

Why you cite/reference

- **Referencing:**
  - Is a systematic way of recording where data and information have been obtained
  - Enables your readers (or your supervisor!) to locate and verify the information presented.
- **Citations:**
  - Are used as a shortened method of making a reference to a source used, placed within the body of the Extended Essay
  - Let you indicate in the essay where you have used the ideas, words or work of someone else.
- The correct use of references and citations is a sign of good-quality academic writing, and also help protect you against potential accusations of plagiarism.

How you cite/reference

- You can choose the citation or referencing style that best suits your needs, but you must use it consistently!
- MLA, APA, Harvard or Chicago are the common reference styles.
- Most referencing styles include (more or less) all of the same elements:
  - Author
  - Title
  - Date of publication
  - Date of access
  - Publisher
  - Pages
  - URL (for online sources).
- Use quotation marks if you are using the exact words of another person.

referencing

What you cite/reference

- As well as text sources, make sure you acknowledge audio-visual materials, diagrams, images, graphs, data tables and other illustrations.
- At the end of your essay you must list the sources of all your citations on a separate page. This is known as a bibliography.
- Remember, cite as you write! Make sure you note down all your citations as you write – you will find it hard to remember all your sources otherwise.

Resources

- If you find yourself struggling with citations and referencing, consider using online tools to help. EasyBib and RefMe are two tools you might find useful:
  - **www.refme.com/**
  - **www.easybib.com/**
- For more detailed information on styles for citations and referencing refer to the IB document *Effective citing and referencing*. Find it in the IB's Online Curriculum Centre, or download it here: **goo.gl/YqvYc5.**
- Remember, if in doubt, ask your supervisor, the Extended Essay Coordinator and/or your school Librarian for further guidance!

5 Citation and referencing

Introduction to citation and referencing

Academic honesty is integral to all IB programmes. As the Extended Essay (EE) is a highly academic piece of work, you are expected to acknowledge the ideas, opinions, words or works of other people. Failing to do so may be considered as academic malpractice. For this reason, the IB states that candidates must acknowledge all sources used for the work submitted for assessment, including the EE.

Citation and referencing are important when writing for an academic audience, as with the EE. In the process of producing your EE, you may end up using a variety of media, textbooks, academic journals, DVD documentaries, statistical tables and graphs, photos, illustrations, images and online sources. Irrespective of the medium, when you use the works, ideas or creations of someone else, you must acknowledge the source using a standard referencing style which is applied in a consistent way.

Very importantly, proper citation and referencing will protect you against any potential accusations of plagiarism, that is, taking credit for other people's work, whether intentional or not. This can, in the worst-case scenario, lead to the disqualification of a candidate because of confirmed academic malpractice (dishonesty). However, the main reason for citation and referencing (C&R) is more than just academic honesty as it is about good quality academic writing. Indeed, C&R should be used to establish your credentials as an academic writer. Ultimately, the proper use of C&R helps you, your EE supervisor and the EE examiner.

It is important to note that whilst teachers and supervisors are strongly encouraged to provide you with advice on how to cite and reference, they are not allowed to correct your biographies or citations.

> **EXPERT TIP**
>
> Failure to acknowledge all the sources used in your essay is a potential breach of the IB's regulations. See Chapter 4 for more details about academic honesty.

The IB's minimum requirements

As stated, the IB does not prescribe a particular system for citation and referencing. However, for reasons of academic honesty, the minimum requirements for the EE include:

- The title of the source
- The name of the author(s)
- The publication date
- Page numbers (for print sources)
- Date of access (for electronic sources).

You should also include references to any interviews, stating:

- The name of the interviewee
- The date of the interview
- The venue of the interview.

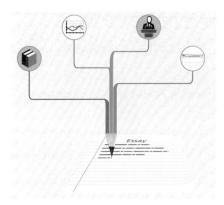
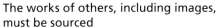

The works of others, including images, must be sourced

All sources must be properly and consistently referenced

In addition, whichever style you decide to use, you are expected to apply this in a consistent way. The ideas, arguments or works of others must be credited to the source. This includes the use of paraphrasing or summarizing the work of others. Essentially, this means you must clearly distinguish between your own words used in the essay and those of others.

Don't worry too much about having to create a flawless referencing system for your EE. You are, however, expected to show that *all* sources have been properly acknowledged. Therefore, this includes acknowledging audio-visual materials, diagrams, images, graphs, data tables and other illustrations in addition to any texts you have used.

EXPERT TIP

Remember, *all* sources must be properly referenced in the bibliography, so that the examiner can trace the source if need be.

COMMON MISTAKE

Too often, students rely purely on subject-specific textbooks or online sources for their research. Remember that examiners look for a range of reliable and relevant sources so you can critically assess and support your arguments and conclusions.

EXPERT TIP

Try to think of academic writing as an academic conversation or debate. As the author, you present a possible answer to the research question but must argue and justify your case to an audience. To do this, you must use relevant examples and evidence from other people's work to support your case. You want the best witnesses possible, so cite and reference these.

What are citations?

Citations are used as a shortened method of making a reference to a source used, placed within the body of the EE. You can use in-text citations, footnotes or endnotes. Despite its brevity, a citation must provide the supervisor and examiner with sufficient information to locate the source. As a condensed or summarized form of acknowledging your sources, all citations must be fully referenced in a bibliography (works cited) at the end of your essay.

The IB does not prescribe a particular citation or referencing style, so you are free to choose one that best suits your needs. For the purpose of academic writing, in-text citations appear next to the quotation or paraphrased text you have written, and should include the page number if you have used a quotation from a print source:

(Author's Last Name Page Number)

This can be done in more than one way. For example:

- Romantic poetry is characterized by the "spontaneous overflow of powerful feelings" (Wordsworth 263).

- Wordsworth stated that Romantic poetry was "a spontaneous overflow of powerful feelings" (263).

If you are using an author–date citation style, then you need the date as well.

Take the following examples from John Royce's article in *IB Review* magazine, published by Hodder Education. Each of the examples contains the same quotation from Kahneman, D. (2011). *Thinking fast and slow*. London: Allen Lane. However, each example uses a different form citing the quotation, but adds authority to the original author and credibility to your own work.

- It may be human nature to think that we are more astute than we really are, to see what we want to see and to ignore that which might work against us. It could be that, "More often than not, risk takers underestimate the odds they face, and do not invest sufficient effort to find out what the odds are." (Kahneman, 2011, p. 256).

- … As Kahneman puts it, "More often than not, risk takers underestimate the odds they face, and do not invest sufficient effort to find out what the odds are" (2011, p. 256).

- … Kahneman's research (2011) suggests that "More often than not, risk takers underestimate the odds they face, and do not invest sufficient effort to find out what the odds are" (p. 256).

- … In 2011, behavioural economist Daniel Kahneman suggested "More often than not, risk takers underestimate the odds they face, and do not invest sufficient effort to find out what the odds are" (p. 256).

- … Daniel Kahneman, awarded the Nobel Prize for Economics in 2002, has shown that "More often than not, risk takers underestimate the odds they face, and do not invest sufficient effort to find out what the odds are" (2011, p. 256).

Source: Royce, John. "Citation and Referencing." *IB Review*, vol.2, no.4, Hodder Education, April 2016, pp. 13–15.

Citation is relatively easy as there are fewer things to remember than there are with referencing. For purposes of academic honesty, all you need is to indicate in the essay where you have used the ideas, words or work of someone else. Use quotation marks if you are using the exact words of another person.

Finally, it is important to remember that all citations should be fully referenced on a works cited or bibliography page. For example:

In-text citation	Works Cited page
One distinguished anthropologist calls the American male's reluctance to cry "a lessening of his capacity to be human" (Montagu 248).	Montagu, Ashley. *The American Way of Life.* New York: Putnam, 1967.

The full citation should appear in an alphabetical list at the end of your EE (bibliography) on a separate page. The bibliographic information in the works cited page(s) must allow the examiner (reader) to locate your sources.

It pays dividends to cite as you write your essay

For example:

■ Hoang, Paul. *Economics for the IB Diploma: Revision Guide*. Hodder Education, 2014.

■ Taylor, Chris. *Riding the Dragon: A Journey Through Every Chinese Province*. CreateSpace, 2013.

■ Wordsworth, William. *Lyrical Ballads*. Oxford University Press, 1967.

What is referencing?

Movies often include a long list of credits at the end. Novels often include acknowledgements at the beginning or end. Artwork and music may include attribution in the title (Portrait of a Lady, after Klimt, or Variations on a Theme by Joplin). A poster or collage might include an outline of the pieces used and a note on the source used for each. Referencing is used to attribute your sources.

Referencing is a systematic way of recording where data and information have been obtained. It is used to acknowledge the ideas of other people. It also enables your supervisor to locate and verify the information presented. You must provide a full reference whenever you use or refer to the work, ideas and arguments of other people. This could, for example, be a quote from a textbook, novel, magazine, academic journal, newspaper or website.

Although there are no specific rules set by the IB, you must use a single referencing style (such as MLA, APA, Harvard or Chicago) consistently throughout your work. If you conduct primary research, such as interviews and/or questionnaires (to supplement your secondary data sources), you must reference these sources too.

You are not expected to be an expert in citation and referencing for academic purpose, but you are expected to acknowledge all sources in a consistent way.

COMMON MISTAKE

Many students think that they can write their 4,000-word EE without the use of citations or references, and then revisit what they have written by adding C&R at a later date. This approach is highly ineffective and inefficient as students usually find it difficult or tedious to locate their sources and/or distinguish between the works and words of others and those of their own.

Choosing an appropriate referencing style

Which (type of) referencing style should you use? The IB does not prescribe a certain referencing style, so this is left at the discretion of your school and IB Diploma Coordinator. You should check whether there is a specific policy (or preference) at your school.

Nevertheless, the different referencing styles all use (more or less) the same elements:

- Author
- Title
- Date of publication
- Date of access

- Publisher
- Pages
- URL (for online sources).

It is the punctuation that is different in different referencing styles, and the order in which the elements are included in the reference. For most people, it is best to stick to one referencing style and get to know that well as it is easy to be confused by the requirements of different types of referencing styles.

EXPERT TIP

Your supervisor is instructed to authenticate your work before the essay is uploaded for assessment. This cannot be done if your supervisor thinks there are shortcomings in citations or referencing, which could suggest plagiarism or academic malpractice.

Do not worry about citation and referencing having a negative impact on your 4,000-word count. The use of C&R, whether they appear as parenthesis, footnotes or endnotes, does not form part of the word count. Instead, focus on providing the reader with precise and accurate citations and reference.

Below are examples of C&R from three different styles: APA, MLA and CMS.

▣ The APA style

Some – but not all – journals in some of the natural sciences and the social sciences use an author-date style, such as **APA** (the style guide of the American Psychological Association). Some examples are provided below.

Media	In-text citation	Works Cited (Bibliography) page
Book	(Passer & Smith, 2015)	Passer, M. W., & Smith, R. E. (2015). *Psychology: The science of mind and behaviour* (2nd ed.). North Ryde, NSW: McGraw-Hill Education.
Image	(Van Gogh, 1888)	Van Gogh, V. (1888). Van Gogh's Chair [Painting]. London: The National Gallery.
Online newspaper (no author)	("Volkswagen plans 30,000 job cuts worldwide", 2016)	*Volkswagen plans 30,000 job cuts worldwide.* (2016). Retrieved from http://www.bbc.com/news/business-38023933

In most cases, your sources should be contemporary in nature. Including dates in writing your essay can be important, and it helps the examiner to know immediately about the recency of your sources, rather than the reader having to look up the date in the references list or bibliography at the end.

For more information about using the APA style, visit their website: **www.apastyle.org/products/asc-for-students.aspx** or watch this short YouTube video: **goo.gl/S3BNL9**.

▣ The MLA style

Some – but not all – journals in language and literature use an author style, such as **MLA** (the style guide of the Modern Language Association). It seems not to matter when the source said or wrote the words, it is the name of the source which gives authority. If you feel that the date is important, you can still include it in the text.

An example adapted from the MLA *Formatting and Style Guide* is shown below. 'Core elements' are the basic pieces of information that are common to all sources, from books to articles, lectures to tweets. Include as many of the core elements as possible when referencing.

	Core Element	Example
1	Author's name.	Royce, John.
2	Title of source.	"Citation and Referencing."
3	Title of container,	*IB Review,*
4	Other contributors,	
5	Version (Edition),	
6	Number,	vol. 2, no.4,
7	Publisher,	Hodder Education,
8	Date of publication,	April 2016,
9	Location. (page number)	pp.13–15.
9	Location (website address <…>)	<www.hoddereducation.com>

So, with the core elements above, the full reference becomes:

Royce, John. "Citation and Referencing." *IB Review*, vol.2, no.4, Hodder Education, April 2016, pp. 13–15.

▪ The CMS style

Some – but not all – journals in history and other humanities subjects use a footnoting style, such as **CMS** (Chicago Manual of Style or simply **Chicago**, for short), the style guide of the University of Chicago Press. This style is preferred by some readers because the use of parenthetical citations within the text of the EE may slow down the reader. The CMS style uses superscript or bracketed numbers in the text, indicating the reference at the foot of the page (footnote) or at the end of the EE (endnote). Some examples are shown in the table below:

Media	Footnote examples	Works Cited (Bibliography) page
Book	11. Aravind Adiga, *The White Tiger* (Uttar Pradesh, India: HarperCollins, 2009), 165.	Adiga, Aravind. *The White Tiger*. Uttar Pradesh, India: HarperCollins, 2009
Journal	12. Sian May, "What is freedom?" *IB Review*, vol. 3 no. 3 (2017): 15.	May, Sian. "What is freedom?" *IB Review*, vol. 3 no. 3 (2017): 14–17.
Website	15. Eric Ng, "Chinese exporters gain from weak yuan while dollar debtors, importers take a hit," *South China Morning Post*, November 18, 2016, accessed June 14, 2017, http://www.bbc.com/news/business-38020900	Ng, Eric. "Chinese exporters gain from weak yuan while dollar debtors, importers take a hit." *South China Morning Post*, November 18, 2016. Accessed June 14, 2017. http://www.bbc.com/news/business-38020900

For more information about using the CMS style, visit their website: http://www.chicagomanualofstyle.org/tools_citationguide.html.

> **EXPERT TIP**
>
> For the EE, any style can be used for any subject, as long as it is used consistently.

▪ Using and referencing online materials

Increasingly, students are using online materials as sources for their EE. Whichever referencing system is used, it is important to include, as a minimum, the following information:

- The title of the online material used
- The (full) website address
- The date it was accessed
- The author (if available).

> **EXPERT TIP**
>
> As citation and referencing are not part of the word count, there is no need to use software, such as Google URL Shortener. Instead, use the full URL website address.

For example, you may choose to use the following format:

Author's Last Name, First Name. "Article title." *Name of website source.* Publisher. Date of article listed on site. <URL: www.>

Example:

Eder, Steve. "Donald Trump Agrees to Pay $25 Million in Trump University Settlement." *New York Times,* November 19, 2016. <URL: www.nytimes.com/2016/11/19/us/politics/trump-university.html?ref=business>

If the online source contains page numbers, such as a PDF online report, the relevant page(s) should also be included in the referencing.

It is also important to note that online materials must be used with some caution – you should use and rely only on reputable sources. In particular, you should consider the following points:

■ Judge the reliability and validity of the information found online – for example, how trustworthy is the source?

■ Do not rely solely on internet sources – your bibliography should not contain only online sources.

■ Having a sharply focused research question will help you to search better for relevant materials on the internet.

Online materials must be used with some caution

Being able to think critically is assessed in Criterion C, which is worth 12 out of the 34 marks for the EE. See Chapter 8 for more information about showing evidence of critical thinking in your essay.

The standard format and presentation of the EE includes the requirement of proper citation and referencing. Many students find this task to be challenging, despite its importance. There is plenty of freely available software on the internet to help you with this task. You basically need to get into the habit of citing and referencing the materials and ideas that are not your own. This includes the proper C&R of images, graphs, charts, tables and diagrams.

■ Final words of advice

Many students use an inconsistent referencing style within their essay. You should speak with your supervisor, the EE Coordinator and/or school Librarian about using a recognized style for citation and referencing.

If you find yourself struggling with C&R, consider using online tools to help. EasyBib and RefMe are two useful tools for C&R:

- **www.refme.com/**
- **www.easybib.com/**

Finally, for more detailed information on styles for citations and referencing please refer to the IB document 'Effective citing and referencing', available for download (**http://goo.gl/QLTGVC**) and on the IB's Online Curriculum Centre – ask your EE supervisor for a copy.

EXPERT TIP

Proper use of citations and references can help you to gain marks under Criterion E – Engagement. This criterion assesses the depth of your reflections, demonstrating the degree of your engagement with the learning process. Citations and referencing are important skills that you can demonstrate you have learned.

CHAPTER SUMMARY KEY POINTS

- Referencing is used to acknowledge and credit the work of others cited in your essay.

- Use citation and referencing when referring to the work, words or thoughts of others.

- Citations in the text of your EE show that you are being academically honest. Referencing is an integral aspect of academic honesty.

- Failure to acknowledge your sources is a potential breach of the IB's regulations, so will be investigated. This can result in a penalty imposed by the IB's Final Award Committee, including disqualification.

- Good use of citation and referencing helps you show off your research and writing skills in the EE.

- The references you use help to add strength to your arguments, by improving the analysis of your research in the context of the essay.

- Record your sources throughout the process of your research and writing, rather than trying to construct a list of all the sources at the end of the process.

■ END OF CHAPTER QUIZ

	Question	True	False
1	EE examiners must be able to trace each of your sources by following the referencing system you have used.	■	■
2	Citation and referencing are important in the EE because the essay is targeted at an academic audience.	■	■
3	It is important that you acknowledge all contributing sources in your essay.	■	■
4	You must use a referencing system that is prescribed by the IBO.	■	■
5	You can use footnotes or endnotes for citations and references.	■	■
6	You should use an academic referencing style as soon as you start writing your essay, because it becomes more difficult to add these at a later date.	■	■
7	If used, primary data sources (such as interviews and questionnaires) must be referenced.	■	■
8	You must provide a full list of works cited and references in a bibliography.	■	■
9	When using online sources, it is necessary to include the date of the article but not the date it was accessed.	■	■
10	Only your supervisor is permitted to assist you with citation and referencing.	■	■

What you can expect from your supervisor

- Your supervisor will:
  - Provide three to five hours of overall support
  - Complete three compulsory reflection sessions with you (during which your supervisor will sign and date your RPPF)
  - Read and provide feedback on the first draft of your Extended Essay
  - Monitor your progress to offer guidance and ensure that the essay is your own work
  - Check your essay does not reuse any work that you have completed for a previous assessment
  - Ensure that you fully understand the significance of academic honesty issues
  - Read the final version of your essay to confirm its authenticity
  - Submit a predicted grade (mark) for your completed essay, out of 34 marks, and write the supervisor's comments on page 3 of the RPPF
  - Upload your Extended Essay to IBIS.

Essay supervisor

What you can expect from your supervisor sessions

- The three compulsory reflection sessions are a formal part of the Extended Essay and will be recorded on the Reflections on Planning and Progress Form (RPPF).

- Each reflection session should last between 20 to 30 minutes. They will:
  - Focus on the progress made so far
  - Set clear objectives for moving forward
  - The third reflection session is the *viva voce*, an opportunity to talk about your engagement with researching and writing the essay.

- You should be fully prepared for these meetings.
  - Consider creating a Researcher's Reflection Space (RRS) – this can be used as stimulus material during reflection sessions.

- REMEMBER – the three reflection meetings are <u>not</u> the only times that you should see your supervisor.
  - Additional check-in meetings should last around ten minutes.
  - You should meet as necessary and receive a minimum of three hours of supervision.

6 The role of the Extended Essay supervisor

The supervisor is vital to the whole process of writing an Extended Essay (EE). Your supervisor has several important administrative jobs to do:

- Provide you with three to five hours of support (including the time needed for the three compulsory reflection meetings).

- Conduct the three compulsory reflection sessions with you (see Chapter 7 for more details). You will need to complete the Reflections on Planning and Progress Form (RPPF) and this needs to be signed and dated by your supervisor.

- Read and comment on one draft only, but note that supervisors are not allowed to edit the draft. Altering any part of your work is potentially academic malpractice.

- Provide you with feedback on the first (and only) draft of your essay. This should take place after the interim reflection meeting, but must be before the *viva voce* (the final reflection meeting).

- Monitor the progress of the EE process in order to offer guidance and to ensure that the essay is your own work.

- Make sure that your essay does not reuse any work that you have completed for assessment in any other component, such as an Internal Assessment. This would otherwise constitute academic dishonesty.

- Ensure that you fully understand the significance of academic honesty issues, especially regarding rules about plagiarism and respect for intellectual property. Your supervisor will need to submit a written report to your school's IB Diploma Programme Coordinator if academic misconduct, such as plagiarism, is suspected in the final draft of your essay. See Chapter 4 for more guidance on academic honesty and the EE.

- Read the final version of your essay to confirm its authenticity.

- Submit a predicted grade (mark) for your completed essay, out of 34 marks, and write the supervisor's comments on page 3 of the RPPF. Your supervisor should write meaningful comments as examiners do read these statements.

- Upload your EE to IBIS.

> **EXPERT TIP**
>
> Your supervisor is able to gain access to copies of relevant IB publications that are available on the Programme Resource Center (PRC). These publications include exemplar essays and EE subject reports. Ask your supervisor to share these with you.

Your supervisor is your best support

The role of the supervisor is undoubtedly much more than purely administrative. Although a supervisor is not permitted to edit your work, a good supervisor will guide and advise you all through the entire EE journey, including the reflection sessions. They will also prove invaluable during the planning stage, when you are carrying out and writing up your research for the essay. Very importantly, the relationship you have and build with your supervisor will be one of the most important aspects of the whole process.

Your supervisor will be a suitably qualified member of staff at the school in which your EE subject is registered. Hence, you should make good use of your supervisor, a subject expert, in helping you to make good choices, and to plan and conduct your research.

Supervision is an important and challenging task, though it doesn't require SUPER VISION

The student–supervisor relationship is a vital aspect in the Extended Essay process

Your supervisor is there to encourage and support you as well as to keep the essay on track in terms of formal and official requirements. You should aim to develop a really good working relationship with your supervisor and the best way to do this is to be proactive and organized in communication and with developing your own ideas for writing the essay.

Your supervisor will need to provide an explanation in cases where the number of hours spent with a candidate is less than the stipulated minimum three hours, especially how it has been possible to guarantee the authenticity of the essay in such circumstances.

> **EXPERT TIP**
>
> Be proactive from the start in your relationship with your supervisor. Don't attend the first meeting with only a couple of ideas about the direction of your essay – impress your supervisor with your thinking and preparation in order to make the first meeting go well.

> **EXPERT TIP**
>
> Remember that your supervisor is only permitted to spend three to five hours in total with you on the EE, so you must use this time wisely and ask good questions.

Supervisor reflection sessions

There are three compulsory reflection sessions that are a formal part of the EE. These reflection sessions should focus on the progress you have made so far and set clear objectives for moving forward. All three reflection sessions must be recorded on the RPPF, and then signed and dated by your supervisor for authentication purposes. On completion of the *viva voce*, your supervisor will then add his/her own written comments.

As the reflection sessions are formally assessed, you should be fully prepared for these meetings. Note that the IB recommends each reflection session to last between 20 to 30 minutes, with your supervisor guiding you through a series of questions (again, see Chapter 7 for further guidance on this).

Following the completion of all three reflection sessions, your RPPF will be submitted to the International Baccalaureate along with your completed EE. Make sure you and your supervisor both sign this form – if it is not signed by both parties, it may result in a delay in a grade being issued for the EE and possibly lower marks awarded for Criterion E (engagement).

> **EXPERT TIP**
>
> You may find it useful to have a Researcher's Reflection Space (RRS). You can then use the RRS as stimulus material during the three formal reflection sessions, and share extracts from the RRS with your supervisor. See Chapter 7 for more details about using a RRS.

Supervising (guiding) your supervisor

When you have your reflection sessions with your supervisor, make sure you are fully prepared and focused on the part you need to play in this process. Consider the questions that would be useful for you to ask in order to make further progress with your essay.

It is also useful for you to be aware of what your supervisor will be doing during these compulsory reflection sessions and what they will bear in mind as they conduct the conversations with you. Some considerations for you to prepare for, include the following points:

- Your supervisor will need to work out what progress you have made and how your essay is taking shape.

- Your supervisor will be aware that the RPPF is an assessed part of the EE. The supervisor's comments must include reflections of the discussions with you during the mandatory reflection sessions. They must also include a comment about your overall level of engagement throughout the EE process.

- Examiners, and hence your supervisor, will want to know that you understand the materials (which must be properly referenced) you have included in your essay. If this is not the case, your supervisor will check your understanding during the *viva voce* and comment on this in the RPPF.

- Similarly, examiners and hence your supervisor will check for academic honesty issues. The supervisor cannot authenticate an essay if they believe the candidate is guilty of plagiarism or some other form of academic misconduct. For example, if there appear to be major shortcomings in citations or referencing, the supervisor will investigate this thoroughly.

- Unless there are particular problems, your supervisor will want the *viva voce* to begin and end positively. You should remember that completion of a challenging and key piece of work, such as the EE, is a major achievement for you, so your supervisor will want to recognize this!

> **EXPERT TIP**
>
> With the IB's requirement for the anonymization of all coursework, your supervisor's comments won't refer to you by name but as 'the candidate'. Similarly, your comments cannot reveal who you are or which school you attend.

■ Other sessions with your supervisor

The three mandatory reflection meetings are not the only times that you should see your supervisor. In fact, you should meet with your supervisor as necessary (remember that each reflection session should last up to 30 minutes, yet you should receive a minimum of three hours of supervision).

The regularity and length of these additional meetings will depend on your individual needs and how satisfied your supervisor is with your level of progress. Typically lasting about ten minutes, these additional sessions will check, clarify and confirm both your progress and your next steps. During these meetings you can, of course, also ask your supervisor questions regarding any matters you are not sure about.

These additional check-in meetings with your supervisor are not part of the formal reflection sessions, so nothing needs to be recorded on your RPPF.

Although it is your EE, your supervisor will be able to give you advice and support in order to develop ideas and research methods. Experienced supervisors understand that the key to a successful EE stems from the planning and research stage, so will be able to guide you before you put pen to paper.

The vast majority of the essay is in the pre-writing/draft phase when you and your supervisor work together to:

- Explore and discuss ideas for topic development
- Discuss and locate suitable resources
- Discuss readings and ideas for developing the essay
- Construct a suitable research question.

The rest of the essay is in the writing phase when you work independently to:

- Write the complete EE first draft
- Make any necessary alterations following the interim reflection session with your supervisor
- Prepare and write the final draft of the EE.

This is a bit like an iceberg. The completed essay is what the examiner sees but the majority of the work involves research and planning 'behind the scenes'. The examiner does not see this but it is impossible to have a completed EE without it. The supervisor's role is to assist and advise with this process.

■ The role of the Librarian supervisor

Don't forget the role of the Librarian as a 'supervisor'. The EE guide says that supervisors are expected to advise you about:

- Accessing suitable and appropriate resources to conduct the necessary research for the essay
- Research methodologies
- Citation and referencing.

Most of your hard work with the EE is beneath the surface and never seen by the examiner

Your Librarian is a super Extended Essay resource, so make good use of them!

Your school's Librarian will have expertise in the above, and will be able to support you with research and referencing skills as you write your essay. Your school might arrange dedicated talks (perhaps in assemblies or lessons) with the Librarian to lead such sessions. Alternatively, you can seek help on an individual basis by asking your Librarian for assistance.

Supervisor do's and don'ts

Your supervisor is permitted to show you how your essay can be improved. Your supervisor can do this by using open-ended comments but must not edit any of your work. For example, your supervisor may ask how you think you can make some of your arguments clearer or more convincing, or ask if you think there is anything missing (a hint that there might be!). They might also give you advice on your citations and references, indicate if there are inconsistencies in the essay that need to be reviewed, or suggest you check your calculations (if used).

In line with the expectation of academic honesty, supervisors cannot make changes to your written work. For instance, they must not correct your spelling, punctuation and grammar, nor must they rewrite any part of your essay – doing so means it potentially no longer represents your ideas or work. Similarly, for Science and Mathematics essays, your supervisor must not correct or change any of your experimental work or calculations.

As no student is allowed to gain an unfair advantage over others, your supervisor must not repeatedly look at your essay, even if it means looking at sections of your work. In fact, your supervisor is not permitted to read or comment on more than one draft of your essay – even if it isn't a full draft. The second time you submit your essay must be the final version of the work.

> **EXPERT TIP**
>
> Remember that your supervisor can only look at one complete draft of your essay. Therefore, make sure you attend all scheduled meetings with your supervisor to ensure you stay on track to completing a full first draft essay. This will enable your supervisor to provide more meaningful feedback.

■ Supervisor comments on your draft essay

Commenting on one draft of your essay is a very important part of the latter stages of your EE. As it is essentially the last point at which the supervisor sees the essay before it is finally uploaded for submission, it is vital that your draft is a complete one. Note that your supervisor will be aware that s/he has to provide the right level of support. Not enough support (less than three hours) can mean you do not write to the best of your ability and the supervisor may not be able to authenticate the work. Providing you with too much support (more than five hours) means the essay may not be entirely your own work or you may not have completed the essay as an independent learner.

After submitting the first (and only) draft of the essay, you should set up a time for a one-to-one discussion with your supervisor in order to get feedback and advice on what can be improved. Your supervisor is allowed to give you plenty of advice, but s/he will know that they cannot heavily annotate your work, nor can they edit any part of your essay.

> **EXPERT TIP**
>
> A common shortcoming of many EEs is a weak conclusion. Too often, students write conclusions that are inconsistent with the research conducted or leave the research question unanswered. This seems like a careless omission, and it probably is, so make sure you don't do this!

■ The supervisor's role in the *viva voce*

> *Viva Voce*
>
> The *viva voce* is your opportunity to explain your engagement with the essay to your supervisor

Viva voce derives from Medieval Latin, where it literally translates as 'with the living voice'. This means that your *viva voce* is an oral examination of your work on the EE. Your supervisor will use the *viva voce* to gain a good idea of how you have tackled your research question and what you have learned from writing this major piece of work. It is the third and final reflection session, and allows your supervisor to do a final check for plagiarism; after all, the supervisor must be able to authenticate your work.

The recommended duration of the *viva voce* is between 20 and 30 minutes. Note that this reflection session is included as part of the recommended amount of supervision time (three to five hours).

After the *viva voce*, your supervisor will need to complete the RPPF and make a judgement about your overall level of engagement with the whole EE process. You can also expect questions about your understanding of the essay and the material that you have used. Naturally, some of the comments made by your supervisor on the RPPF will relate to this.

Your supervisor is not trying to do the examiner's job during the *viva voce*, but should try to point out to the examiner what aspects of the essay you have engaged with particularly well. The *viva voce* is an opportunity for you to celebrate your success and highlight your level of commitment. Don't pass this opportunity up! Use the *viva voce* as your 'living voice' in order to let your supervisor know how you have engaged with the various tasks in completing the EE. This will enable your examiner to also know.

Some typical questions that you might expect from your supervisor during the *viva voce* include:

■ General questions

- Why did you decide on this particular research question?
- What did you find to be the most interesting aspect of your research?
- How did your thinking about this topic develop as you went through this research process?
- Now that you have completed the essay, which part of the process would you say you enjoyed most and why?
- Were there any surprises along the way?
- How have you developed as a researcher having gone through this process?

- ■ Research context
  - You refer to ... as a key influence on your research – can you summarize the particular relevance of their work?
  - What developments have there been in this field (topic) since you began your essay?
  - You make only passing reference to ... – why do you think that this is less relevant than the others you have given more priority to?
  - You do not say much about ... in your essay – can you explain why you did not focus more on that?

- ■ Research methods
  - Did you have any problems with the data collection process?
  - How well did your methodology work in reality?
  - What were the main ethical issues or considerations when conducting your research?
  - How did you establish the limits around the scope of your data collection?

- ■ Analysis and findings
  - Can you talk me through your methods of analysis?
  - Did you encounter any problems with applying these methods of analysis?
  - Do you think the data you collected were the most appropriate to answer your research question or are there any other data you would have liked to have collected?
  - Can you describe your main findings in a few sentences?

- ■ Discussion
  - If you were starting your research again now, are there any changes in the way you would plan it?
  - You interpret these findings as ... but do you think there could be an argument for interpreting them as ... instead?
  - You said in your essay that ... – can you expand on that point?
  - In what ways do you consider your essay to be original?

- ■ Conclusions/implications
  - What are the empirical and theoretical implications of your findings?
  - How would you hope that this research could be followed up and taken further?

EXPERT TIP

When completing the RPPF, be aware that your supervisor must comply with the IB's requirement for the anonymization of all EEs. Hence, your supervisor's comments must not refer to you by name but as 'the candidate'.

CHAPTER SUMMARY KEY POINTS

- Your supervisor has several important administrative jobs to do.

- Your supervisor will offer a minimum of three hours and up to a maximum of five hours of support. This includes the three formal reflection sessions.

- Your supervisor will read and provide you with feedback on the first (and only) draft of the EE, but is not permitted to edit the draft.

- The school Librarian is an important person to give guidance on research and referencing, and the formatting of the essay.

- Your supervisor will submit and authenticate your essay and the RPPF to the IBO for assessment by an examiner.

- The *viva voce* is an opportunity to talk to the supervisor about your engagement with researching and writing the essay.

■ END OF CHAPTER QUIZ

	Question	True	False
1	The supervisor is advised to spend no longer than 6 hours with each student.	■	■
2	The supervision time includes the three compulsory reflection sessions on planning and progress.	■	■
3	Your supervisor is allowed to edit and annotate **one** completed draft of your essay.	■	■
4	*Viva voce* translates as 'with a living voice' and should last for one hour.	■	■
5	The *viva voce* is included in the total time that the supervisor should spend with the candidate.	■	■
6	The supervisor must not correct the spelling, punctuation or grammar in your essay.	■	■
7	Supervisors are allowed to support you regarding citations and references.	■	■
8	Your supervisor will refer to you by name on the final RPPF that is submitted to the IB for examiner marking.	■	■
9	Supervisor comments on the draft essay should take place after the interim reflection session but before the final reflection (the *viva voce*).	■	■
10	If you have completed another formal piece of assessment, it is permissible for you to use a similar research question and resources for your EE.	■	■

What is reflection?

- One of the key attributes of an IB learner is to be reflective, considering both the world and your own ideas and experiences as well as supporting your learning and personal development through an understanding of your strengths and weaknesses.
- Reflection is a compulsory part of the Extended Essay and is formally assessed.
- All IB Diploma candidates are required to complete a Reflections on Planning and Progress Form (RPPF) which is sent to the examiner.
- A blank or missing RPPF will score zero marks under assessment Criterion E (engagement).
- The RPPF is worth six marks (almost 18% of the overall marks).

How can I reflect?

The Researcher's Reflection Space (RRS)

- A practical tool you can use to record your thoughts as you write your Extended Essay.
- Helps to develop learning, thinking, critical analysis and evaluation skills.
- The RRS can be an important part of your conversations with your supervisor during the formal reflection meetings.
- Try to use your RRS to think about the following:
  - Planning
  - Research methodology
  - Research findings
  - Decision-making process
  - Setbacks and challenges
  - Areas and actions for improvements.

The Reflections on Planning and Progress Form (RPPF)

- Write your reflective comments on the RPPF as soon as possible after each reflection session while they are still fresh in your mind.
- There is a maximum of 500 words for all three reflection sessions.
- Remember, you must not go back and change or update your reflections at a later date. They are a snapshot of your thinking process throughout the project.

# of reflections

Reflection Sessions

Initial reflection session

WHEN: After your initial ideas, background reading and research plan have been considered.

WHAT TO EXPECT: Questions from your supervisor will be more descriptive in nature, encouraging you to explain and consider your research, reading and thinking.

Ideally send your supervisor an outline of your research plan and progress before this meeting to help ensure your discussion is purposeful and productive.

OUTCOME: You have a good idea of exactly what your research question is and how you are going to deal with the remaining challenges you are likely to face.

Interim reflection session

WHEN: After your draft essay has been submitted.

WHAT TO EXPECT: The session will help you judge how far you have progressed and how much further you will need to go in order to successfully complete the Extended Essay.

There may be more analytical questions from your supervisor, with a discussion of the strengths and limitations of your initial findings and research methods.

OUTCOME: You understand what you have achieved already, and what must still be accomplished, in order to write the best essay you can.

Final reflection session – the *viva voce*

WHEN: After the final version of your Extended Essay has been completed by you, and has been read by your supervisor.

WHAT TO EXPECT: Questions from your supervisor will be more open-ended and evaluative in nature. These will help encourage you to reflect on what you have learned throughout the entire Extended Essay process.

OUTCOME: You have considered and evaluated the wider implications of your learning journey, in particular, you are more self-aware of your personal strengths and academic development needs.

The importance of reflections

What is reflection?

Being reflective is one of the IB learner profile attributes and it has become a formal part of the assessment criteria for the (EE). Under the new assessment model, the Reflections on Planning and Progress Form (RPPF) is worth 6 marks. This is a significant number of marks (almost 18%), which can make the difference between two grades in the final assessment.

Reflection requires us to consider what has happened in order to move forward. For the EE, you should consider the ideas and information collected in order to formulate your own understanding and interpretation of the topic. For instance, you could reflect on the strengths and weaknesses of your experiences in order to further your own learning and personal academic growth.

The previous versions of the EE placed much emphasis on the output of the final essay, without giving students much credit for the process of planning, researching and writing that they went through during their learning journey. The new requirements and assessment criteria address this issue by awarding your ability to reflect on your planning and progress.

As part of the new requirements, you will need to meet with your supervisor to carry out three compulsory reflection sessions. Each of these reflection sessions should last between 20 to 30 minutes, and must be recorded on the RPPF.

EXPERT TIP

Whilst reflections are a new feature of the EE process, they are similar to the reflections that you undertake in Theory of Knowledge (TOK) and Creativity, Activity and Service (CAS). The ability to reflect is a transferable skill.

■ The Researcher's Reflection Space

Before completing the compulsory RPPF, you may want to consider writing a Researcher's Reflection Space (RRS). The most successful students will be able to show that learning is complex and will be able to consider their ideas and actions in response to any setbacks they may have experienced during the research process.

TASK 1

Producing a RRS is a rather like keeping a personal diary to reflect on your day.

1 Write a diary entry about what happened in your life yesterday or last week.

2 Reflect on what went well and what did not go so well.

3 Consider how you might have managed some of these things better.

The RRS is a practical tool you can use to record your thoughts as you write your EE. There are different ways to keep a RRS, such as:

■ Write about what you have read, researched and discovered – a bit like a research log. You should document the whole EE process from the beginning to the end. Your supervisor might ask to see the log as evidence that your research is authentic and/or to help give you further advice.

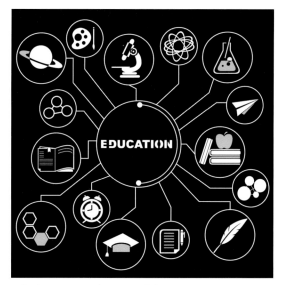

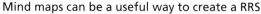

Mind maps can be a useful way to create a RRS

Reflections can help with the many questions you will have during the Extended Essay process

- A process journal – this is where you complete a number of reflections on your learning experiences including obstacles, setbacks and challenges you have faced or are currently facing. You may choose to reflect on certain IB learner profile characteristics to help you overcome challenges or improve your learning experiences.
- Mind mapping – this can be a helpful visual tool to organize and extend your thought processes. Mind maps help learners to show relationships between different pieces of information with the central idea (your research question) in the middle of your page. The use of a mind map can be a useful stimulus for your formal reflection meetings.

All these elements of reflection can be included in your RRS, which can take the form of an online blog or journal, or simply a collection of materials written out and kept in a folder or notebook.

TASK 2

Now that you have chosen a research question for your EE, have a go at producing a RRS for the first part of your research and thinking. You may choose to reflect on the following:

- Your research question
- How you intend to begin your research
- How you intend to collect and select the most relevant source materials
- Anticipated difficulties and how you intend to tackle these
- How you intend to manage your relationship with your supervisor.

Using a RRS can help to develop the learning, thinking, critical analysis and evaluation skills required for scoring well in the EE. In preparing for your three compulsory reflection sessions (for the RPPF), you could use the RRS to record your reflections throughout the process (rather than only during the three compulsory reflection sessions). You can also use your RRS to record your responses and thoughts to different sources, such as news articles, blogs and online social media sources.

Finally, remember that the RRS will form an important part of your conversations with your supervisor during the formal reflection meetings and completion of the RPPF. To prepare for these meetings, try to use your RRS to cover the following thoughts on:

- Planning
- Research methodology
- Research findings
- Decision-making processes
- Setbacks and challenges
- Areas and actions for improvements.

> **EXPERT TIP**
>
> Every successful EE begins with academic curiosity and a research question that you want to find the (possible) answer to, and ends with reflections on the work you have done.

Time management is a vital skill for all students

■ Reflection and Approaches to Learning (ATL)

The ATL skills are essential at various stages in the EE process. Working closely with your supervisor, and using them as a sounding board when **communicating** your ideas and reflections, will also help to develop your **social** skills. The **self-management** needed to complete an independent EE, and the ability to **think critically** about the **research** you have engaged with, are life-long skills that you will continue to use and develop.

Time management is a vital skill for all IB Diploma students, encompassing several of the ATL skills. You might choose to reflect on how the process of writing the EE has helped to develop ATL skills, such as your time management skills, beyond the IB Diploma Programme.

Completing the EE is a very challenging task, especially as most of this must be completed independently (with the support of your supervisor, of course). This means that all five ATL skills become vital if you are to be successful in this component of the IB Diploma Programme.

The RPPF is similar to the Planning and Progress Form (PPF) used for assessing the TOK essay and presentation. You will be aware that the TOK/PPF requires completion of three interactions with your TOK teacher, allowing the examiner to see the development of your ideas through the reflections noted on the form. The purpose and process is the same for the EE.

The Reflections on Planning and Progress Form (RPPF)

The official RPPF must be submitted when you upload your final EE for formal assessment.

A full copy of the form can be found at **www.tinyurl.com/zap34tu**. It is important to note that the RPPF is worth almost 18% of your overall EE grade, a significant number of marks, especially if your overall mark is on the borderline of the next grade up. Therefore, you must ensure that the contents of the RPPF and your essay fit together coherently and consistently.

The focus of reflection in the EE is on the overall process. For each section of the RPPF, consider the following areas for reflection:

- The challenges, setbacks and obstacles you faced – how did you tackle these and what did you learn in the process?
- The IB learner profile – which of these applied to you, and how?
- Your learning experiences – what did you learn and did any new perspectives emerge during the process?

There is a maximum of 500 words for all three reflections. These must be written in your own words and relate only to your own learning journey in this process. You should write your reflective comments on the RPPF as soon as possible after each reflection meeting with your supervisor because these thoughts will still be fresh in your mind. Also, you must not go back and change or update your reflections at a later date – the EE examiner wants to know what you were thinking at that particular moment when each reflection was completed.

It is permitted to change or alter your EE research question even after starting your research and meeting with your supervisor. However, your RRS and RPPF should be an accurate reflection of how your essay has developed and changed and should not be altered retrospectively.

Mandatory reflection sessions

There are three compulsory reflection sessions that must be recorded on the RPPF: the initial reflection, the interim reflection and the *viva voce*. The IB recommends that each of these meetings last between 20 to 30 minutes, focusing on the progress and process of completing the EE. A blank or missing RPPF will mean zero marks under assessment Criterion E (engagement).

You may choose to use your Researcher's Reflection Space (RRS) during these meetings with your supervisor. Following each of the three reflection sessions, you must complete the relevant section of the RPPF (under the column 'Candidate comments') and submit the form to your supervisor for them to date and sign the form.

Initial reflection session

The first reflection session should occur after your initial ideas, background reading and research plan have been considered. These can be recorded in your RRS. You should also have read the subject-specific guidance in the IB *Extended Essay Guide* before this meeting.

> **EXPERT TIP**
>
> It would help your supervisor if you send them an outline of your research plan and progress before the initial reflection meeting. This would give your supervisor a bit of time to examine your work and to prepare a purposeful and productive meeting with you.

Some questions that may arise in this initial conversation, usually of a **descriptive** nature, include:

- Why is the topic/research question appropriate and worthy of study?
- Does your research question need to be modified in light of your initial research?
- How did you undertake the necessary research?
- Were you successful in gathering the data/information/evidence that you wanted?
- Does the data you have collected so far allow you to answer your research question?
- Do you need more sources of information in order to answer your question? Where might you find the data required?
- What were the problems that you faced? How did you tackle these problems?
- Did your approach or methodology change in any way during the process so far?
- What investigations are you undertaking?
- What anticipated difficulties and challenges can you foresee in the next stage of the process? How do you intend to tackle or resolve these challenges?
- Are there any issues or questions emerging from your data collection and research that you did not anticipate?
- What have been the high and the low points of the research process?
- What kind of issues or questions are you going to highlight in your RPPF?

By the end of the initial reflection session, you should have a good idea of exactly what your research question is and how you are going to deal with the remaining challenges you are likely to face.

Remember that you can still see your supervisor for regular check-in sessions in-between the formal reflection sessions. In addition, you can have informal discussions with other people who can help with your research, especially subject specialist teachers, your

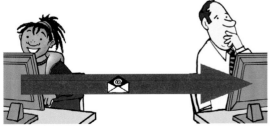
The work doesn't stop between reflection sessions, so keep your supervisor well informed

EE Coordinator and the school Librarian. However, be careful you do not contravene any rules on academic honesty (see Chapter 4).

EXPERT TIP

The first reflection session should focus on questions of a **descriptive** nature, with a maximum of 150 words.

The second reflection session should focus on questions of an **analytical** nature, with a maximum of 150 words.

The final reflection session should focus on questions of an **evaluative** nature, with a maximum of 200 words.

■ Interim reflection session

The second formal reflection session should take place after your draft essay has been submitted. Your essay will address the (clear and refined) research question that both you and your supervisor agreed to commit to. This session will help you judge how far you have progressed and how much further you will need to go in order to successfully complete the EE.

One area you and your supervisor will consider is the progress you have made on citations and referencing (discussed in Chapter 5) for your EE. By this point you should both be satisfied that your essay has a sufficient range of appropriate secondary research sources (as well as any relevant primary research sources that supplement your work).

The questions asked in the interim reflection meeting tend to be more analytical, with a discussion of the strengths and limitations of your initial findings and research methods. Some questions that may arise in this interim conversation, which are usually of an **analytical** nature, include:

- Did you change your approach or methodology during the process? If so, why did you do this?
- How have you critically evaluated the source materials used in producing the draft of your essay?
- What have you learnt from the experience so far in terms of your understanding of the subject area?
- What have you learnt about the skills needed to undertake the research successfully?
- How has your understanding of the topic and research question developed throughout the process so far?
- What will you need to do in order to complete the final draft of your essay?
- What might you need to do in preparation for the final reflection session (the *viva voce*)?

Following the second reflection meeting, as with the initial reflection meeting, you are required to complete the relevant section on the RPPF. You must then submit the official form to your supervisor to sign and date. Remember, whilst you can still make changes before the final submission and reflection session, you cannot adjust your interim reflections on the RPPF after your supervisor has dated and signed the form.

■ Final reflection session – the *viva voce*

The third and final formal reflection meeting can only take place after the final version of your EE has been completed. Your supervisor must have already read the final version of your essay before the *viva voce* can be conducted. You may find it useful to bring along your RRS to this meeting in order to show and discuss how you have grown and developed as a learner throughout this whole process.

> **EXPERT TIP**
>
> The *viva voce* is described by the IB as a 'celebration' of the completion of the EE. So you should celebrate your achievement when the time comes! Your final reflection should therefore include details of how you have really grown and benefitted from the whole experience.

The questions asked in the final reflection session are of an evaluative nature, allowing you to reflect on what you have learned throughout the entire EE process and your supervisor to make a holistic judgement about the extent to which you have engaged in the process. It also enables your supervisor to authenticate the final version of your essay. As with the previous two reflection sessions, the *viva voce* should last around 20 to 30 minutes. This is included in the recommended three to five hours of supervision time. Some questions that may arise in the final reflection conversation, usually of an **open-ended** and **evaluative** nature, include:

■ If you were to do this research question again, what would you do differently and why?

■ Were there any surprises in your learning journey? What did you learn from this?

■ What does success mean to you in the process of producing your EE?

■ To what extent do you think you have been successful in this process?

■ Were the strategies you used for your research question the most appropriate for achieving success?

■ If you used alternative research methodologies and/or subject-specific theories, would this have led to a different outcome?

■ Are there any new or unanswered questions that emerged as a result of your research?

■ What advice would you give to next year's students who have yet to write their EE?

As with all three formal reflection sessions, you must attend the *viva voce* in order to complete the RPPF – an incomplete form will cost valuable marks under assessment Criterion E (engagement). Successfully completing the *viva voce* concludes the whole EE process.

The final reflection meeting encourages you to consider and evaluate the wider implications of your learning journey. Therefore, do not just consider the outcome of your research findings and conclusion, but also how the overall process has made you more self-aware of your personal strengths and academic development needs. Questions to help you with such reflections include:

The *viva voce* is the final step in the Extended Essay process

1 What did I used to think?

2 What do I now think?

3 What happened to change that thinking?

Upon completion of the *viva voce*, your supervisor or EE Coordinator will need to upload the RPPF for formal assessment.

EXPERT TIP

Be fully prepared for each reflection session in order to make the best use of your time and that of your supervisor. Ensure you have read any suggested materials, for example, and be prepared to answer questions based on this. Being unprepared for a formal reflection meeting can raise doubt about a candidate's level of engagement and the authenticity of the work.

EXPERT TIP

Make sure you choose a topic that you are genuinely interested in. This will then allow you to conduct meaningful and in-depth research on your chosen topic. In turn, this makes the overall process more interesting and allows you to carry out more purposeful and effective reflections.

Checklist for student reflections

Do	Don't
Ensure you attend the three compulsory reflection sessions with your supervisor.	Settle for a research question or topic without thinking carefully about what you want to actually address in the essay.
Record your reflections on the RPPF as soon as possible after each reflection session with your supervisor, whilst the ideas and thoughts are fresh in your head.	Make any amendments to the RPPF once your supervisor has signed and dated the form.
Initiate the three reflection sessions with your supervisor.	Be dishonest with your supervisor, as they are there to help you and to authenticate your work.
Initiate check-in meetings (in addition to the formal reflection sessions) with your supervisor if you have any concerns, questions or need further guidance.	View challenges and setbacks as a reason to not reflect well – instead, see these as learning opportunities.
Focus your reflections on: ■ Conceptual understandings ■ Decision-making ■ Engagement with data ■ The research process ■ Time management ■ Methodology ■ Appropriateness of sources ■ Successes and challenges.	Leave it up to your supervisor to chase and motivate you to complete your reflections.
Reflect on any new questions that might have emerged from your research.	Exceed the 500-word limit for the three reflections on the RPPF.
Discuss setbacks and any shifts in direction.	Forget to sign your RPPF after completing each reflection session.

Supervisor responsibilities and the RPPF

Do	Don't
Ensure you conduct the three compulsory reflection sessions with the student.	Formulate the research question for the student as this limits his/her reflections in an authentic way.
Sign and date the RPPF once the student comment has been completed (this authenticates the comment).	Make any changes to the RPPF once you have signed and dated the reflection section on the form.
Discuss setbacks and any shifts in thinking and direction/methodology.	Give your own opinions about the quality of the sources; help the student instead to reflect on the purpose and value of the sources.
Use the online resources and teacher support materials from the IBO to facilitate the reflection sessions.	Tell the student what to write in the RPPF, but do guide them with their reflections.
Keep an eye on the student's overall progress, including regular check-in sessions and not just the compulsory reflection sessions.	Correct the student's work and tell the student what is wrong; instead, help the student to identify and reflect on the issues.
Have a formal meeting/check-in session with the student upon receipt of the first draft.	Allow students to submit multiple drafts as this is not academically honest and hinders authentic reflections.

CHAPTER SUMMARY KEY POINTS

- Being reflective is a vital attribute of the IB learner profile.

- Reflection is a compulsory part of the EE and is formally assessed.

- All IB Diploma candidates are required to complete a Reflections on Planning and Progress Form (RPPF) which is sent to the examiner.

- A blank or missing RPPF will score zero marks under assessment Criterion E (engagement).

- The RPPF is worth six marks (almost 18% of the overall marks).

- You are advised to complete a Researcher's Reflection Space (RRS) to help with the formal reflection sessions and in the completion of the RPPF.

- There are three mandatory reflection sessions with your supervisor:
  - Initial reflection session, with a focus on **descriptive** questions
  - Interim reflection session, with a focus on **analytical** questions
  - Final reflection session (*viva voce*), with a focus on **evaluative** questions.

■ END OF CHAPTER QUIZ

	Question	True	False
1	Being reflective is part of the IB learner profile.	☐	☐
2	Reflection is a compulsory part of the EE.	☐	☐
3	Your supervisor will have three reflection meetings with you.	☐	☐
4	The Reflections on Planning and Progress Form is not sent to the IB for marking.	☐	☐
5	The RPPF must be filled in by you and your supervisor, who must also sign and date the document.	☐	☐
6	Each reflection session should last for about 20 to 30 minutes.	☐	☐
7	There is no word limit on the RPPF.	☐	☐
8	The Researcher's Reflection Space must be completed and will be sent to the IB for assessment.	☐	☐
9	Students are encouraged to change and update their RPPF after discussion with their supervisor.	☐	☐
10	Completion of the *viva voce* completes the whole EE process.	☐	☐

Don't necessarily accept things at face value.

Ask thought-provoking and probing questions.

Seek evidence to substantiate your reasoning and perspectives.

Question whether something might be true.

Question the meaning or validity of something.

Assess the evidence and options presented in order to reach a conclusion.

Show judgement in reaching a reasoned conclusion.

Critical thinking phrases!
Kick start your critical thinking by incorporating these phrases in to your essay:

- On the other hand, …
- However, …
- Despite this, …
- Nevertheless, …
- The most significant point …
- In the short term …, but in the longer term …
- The most important argument …
- The least effective argument …
- The most important point …
- The magnitude of the effect …
- It depends on …

Understanding assessment Criterion C: Critical thinking

Critical thinking is the most significant skill examined in the Extended Essay (EE). It is worth 12 marks out of the 34 marks available for the EE – that's just over 35% (or the equivalent of three grade boundaries!). So what is critical thinking? Thinking about things in a critical way means:

- Not necessarily accepting things at face value
- Asking thought-provoking and probing questions
- Seeking evidence to substantiate your reasoning and perspectives
- Questioning whether something might be true
- Questioning the meaning or validity of something
- Assessing the evidence and options presented in order to reach a conclusion
- Showing judgement and reaching a reasoned conclusion.

Critical thinking skills can be demonstrated by displaying evidence of analysis, discussion and evaluation of the materials and arguments presented in your EE. You must be able to show the examiner that you can judge a situation or an issue, after examining the balance of the evidence you have collected and presented.

Critical thinking is very much about asking (the right) questions

There are rarely right or wrong answers in the EE – all questions, problems or issues can be approached in different ways. Your task is to show that you can address the research question in a balanced way in order to reach a justified conclusion.

For example, essays that are purely summative or descriptive do not add value to an argument, so such an approach does not show good critical thinking. Instead, you should strive to conduct research that generates relevant and purposeful conclusions to be made.

COMMON MISTAKE

Too often, students place their evaluation in a separate section of the essay. Critical thinking skills should be demonstrated throughout the essay, so evaluation should be integrated into the text where appropriate in order to provide insight to an argument, approach, theory or source material that you have referred to.

EXPERT TIP

Although it sounds easy to do, critical thinking requires you to ensure your analysis and discussion points are consistent with the evidence presented.

TASK 1

Critical thinking – a quick quiz

Have a go at these questions to test your critical thinking skills – have a think about the questions before answering and before checking the answers.

1 A cowboy came to town on Friday. He stayed for just two nights and left on Friday. How can this be?

2 What is the smallest three-digit number? (asked by Luke Hoang, aged 8)

3 There were three ripe apples hanging high on a tree. Three people pass by. Each took an apple from the tree, but there were still two left hanging. How can this be?

4 A black dog is crossing a road and a man drives at speed along the same road without his lights on – how does he avoid hitting the dog?

EXPERT TIP

Developing your critical thinking skills is not the same as being critical in a negative way. You will have learnt in Theory of Knowledge (TOK) that there is no such thing as absolute truth. Being a critical thinker means not passively accepting things at face value but to ask useful questions, support your points with evidence, and reason in a coherent manner.

IB LEARNER PROFILE

Be reflective and a thinker

Take a look at this photo and explain what you think is happening:

Some responses could include:
- The laptop is broken.

- The child is overwhelmed by the amount of (home) work she has to complete.
- She is upset about an image on a website.
- She has read a disturbing email or message on social media.

There is no right or wrong answer. Similarly, don't seek to produce a 'right' answer to your research question in the EE. The purpose of this task was to get you to consider:

- Context – contextualized analysis in your essay will help you to gain higher marks for critical thinking
- Assumptions made in your answer – this can help to rule out guesswork
- Justifications for your answer.

When you write your essay, make sure you explain to the examiner the context, assumptions made and reasons (justifications) behind your arguments.

COMMON MISTAKE

Some students seem to think that they can simply compile a list of facts, accompanied by a description of things that have happened. This will not suffice for marks under Criterion C (critical thinking).

EXPERT TIP

You are strongly advised to choose, where possible, one of your Higher Level subjects for the EE. You need to have sufficient depth of subject knowledge and background reading in order to write the essay in a critical way.

Critical thinking and good research questions

Your choice of topic and research question for the EE should enable you to address the issue(s) in a critical manner. Avoid questions that require simple and descriptive responses. These often include titles with the following words:

- What …?
- Who …?
- When …?
- Where …?

Research questions that require analysis, discussion and critical thinking often include the following words:

- To what extent …?
- Should …?
- How significant …?
- Why …?

Take the following examples of titles of a History essay:

1 What were the causes of World War II?

2 What were the most significant causes of the Second World War?

3 To what extent can fascism be blamed for causing World War II?

It should be clear to you that the first question requires a simple, descriptive response to (some of) the causes of the Second World War. Question 2 is better as it requires the candidate to consider which of the causes were the most noteworthy. This would require you to be more analytical and to justify your answer. The third question is the most focused and would require a balanced consideration of why fascism can or cannot be blamed for causing the Second World War. In order to answer this question in a critical way, you would need to consider other factors, such as Japanese militarism and Germany's aggressive foreign policy.

EXPERT TIP

If you are writing an **Economics** EE, please be aware of the **five-year rule**. To allow for critical thinking, your research data must not date back for more than five years. Equally, your Economics research question must not be about an upcoming or theoretical incident. In **History**, there is a **ten-year rule** – any essay focusing on events within the last ten years would not be acceptable.

COMMON MISTAKE

Students who use questionnaires in their essay often say that if they had more time then they would have increased the sample size of their research. The EE should take about 40 hours, so there is plenty of time, including time to plan proper, meaningful primary research, if used.

Critical thinkers do not accept all research information at face value

Source bias

Critical thinkers will aim to minimize bias or inaccuracies in their research sources. Information obtained from your research should not always be accepted at face value. The *Wall Street Journal* reported in November 2016 that a Stanford University study of over 7,800 students revealed that 'most students don't know when news is fake'. Take a look at the article and judge for yourself: **goo.gl/ziYOG7**.

Any source can contain bias or inaccuracies, so good researchers should question the validity of all their research materials. This includes you writing without personal bias too. For example, your conclusion should be derived from the evidence gathered and presented, rather than based on any personal biases or preconceptions.

Your analysis must not rely on a single type of source, that is, don't rely exclusively on textbooks or online sources. Using a suitable range of relevant sources will enable you to better support your own conclusions. Having a variety of viewpoints from an appropriate range of sources will help you to make up your own mind. Asking relevant, probing questions to identify potential bias will also help. For example, you could ask yourself the following:

- Who created the source?
- When was the source created? Is it still up-to-date?
- Who was the resource created for (target audience)?
- Is the creator an expert in the field?
- Does the source provide the whole picture?
- Is there any cultural bias?
- What alternative perspectives are there?

In summary, accurate analysis and credible conclusions must be based on good quality research from sources that are relevant and reputable. The source materials should be analyzed in the body of your essay, highlighting any potential limitations, assumptions and biases. By using a variety of sources to back your arguments, you are more likely to be able to show awareness of contradictory opinions and evidence.

EXPERT TIP

A bibliography (works cited page) is a good indication of whether a candidate has used reputable, reliable and representative sources. See Chapters 3 and 5 for guidance on how to produce a bibliography.

IB LEARNER PROFILE

Open-minded

Critical thinking requires you to be open-minded, free from bias. Consider the two examples below. What do you think when you see these words?

1   *Naja nivea*
2   *Oncosperma horridum*

Answers

1   Many people might associate 'Nivea' with skincare or health products. However, this is the scientific name for a species of poisonous cobra!
2   Similarly, people might associate 'horridum' with something horrible. However, this actually refers to a species of harmless palm tree!

EXPERT TIP

Where appropriate in the essay, consider the potential unreliability of secondary data sources.

Common mistakes with primary research

Where primary research is used in the EE (to supplement the secondary research collected), be careful to avoid these common mistakes:

- Small, unrepresentative sample size used for questionnaires
- Asking irrelevant questions
- No consideration of an appropriate sampling method
- Incomplete transcripts from interviews
- Insufficient evidence of raw primary research data documented in the appendix
- Primary research sources not documented in the works cited (bibliography) page
- Fabricating questionnaire findings.

A word of warning: fabricating research data is not only unethical, it also infringes the IB's stance on academic honesty. Candidates can be disqualified for academic malpractice.

If you choose to present your primary research data using visual tools, such as charts, graphs or tables, make sure these are fully and properly labelled. The data must also be explained or analyzed in order to present and support the argument within the body of the essay.

EXPERT TIP

Be critical of the primary sources you encounter; use your judgement to decide on the validity of what you come across. Take this email as an example, which the authors recently received (Li Ka Shing is one of the wealthiest men in the Asia Pacific region):

From: <info@admin123-info.uk>

Hi,

My name is Li Ka-shing, a philanthropist and the founder of Cheung Kong Holdings and Li Ka Shing Foundation, I am the Chairman of the Board of Hutchison Whampoa Limited (HWL) and Cheung Kong Holdings, the world's largest operator of container terminals and the world's largest health and beauty retailer. We offer support to children through innovative education initiatives. Our core focus is to encourage enterprise through education, training and building the right skills today so our young people can become the entrepreneurs of tomorrow. I believed strongly in 'giving while living.' I had one idea that never changed in my mind – that you should use your wealth to help people and I have decided to give USD$1,200.000.00 (One Million Two Hundred Thousand United State Dollars) to randomly selected individuals worldwide. On receipt of this email, you should count yourself as the lucky individual. Your email address was chosen online while searching at random. Kindly get back to me at your earliest convenience, so I know your email address is valid.

■ Socratic questioning

Socratic questioning is a useful technique that you can use to explore complex issues and ideas encountered in your EE. It can uncover misconceptions and enhance your analysis and evaluation of the research topic.

Critical thinking is improved through the use of questioning to enhance understanding. The technique is derived from classical Greek philosopher Socrates who believed the effective use of questioning promotes active and independent learners. There are six main types of Socratic questions:

■ 1 Questions that seek clarification

- Can you explain that point/answer further?
- What led you to that particular judgement?
- Why did you arrive at that particular conclusion? What made you say that?

■ 2 Questions that challenge

- What assumptions did you make in coming to that conclusion?
- Is there an alternative point of view?
- Is this always the case? Why might there be exemptions to the case?

■ 3 Questions about the evidence

- What evidence have you used to support your arguments?
- In addition to source bias, how might others challenge the evidence you have presented?
- What other information could you have used to help support your research and answer?

■ 4 Questions that consider alternatives

- What might other people think? What different perspectives might they have?
- What possible alternative points of view might there be? Why?
- Could you have approached this from a different angle? Would this have changed your answer/point of view?

■ 5 Questions about implications (consequences)

- What are the short-term implications of this?
- Do these implications differ from the long-term consequences?
- How do the outcomes impact on different individuals and societies?

■ 6 Questioning the questions

- What questions did you ask, and why did you ask those questions?
- What was the importance of the questions you asked?
- What additional questions might you have asked?

EXPERT TIP

In essence, you are more likely to be able to show evidence of critical thinking in your EE if you can use Socratic questioning. By doing so, you can often analyze and evaluate your research question at a much higher level.

Writing purposeful conclusions

The purpose of a conclusion is to summarize and synthesize your responses to the research question. To score well for your conclusion, make sure you follow these guidelines. In particular, your conclusion must:

- Synthesize the arguments presented in the body of the essay
- Present a well-thought-out evaluation of the research question based on the research gathered and the discussions in the essay
- Answer the research question, that is, state what has been achieved
- Be consistent with the data, analysis and supporting evidence presented in the essay
- Include any limitations and any unresolved questions.

The conclusion must not:

- Only repeat or summarize what has already been presented before in the essay (the research question must be answered)
- Contain personal bias or unjustified opinions
- Introduce new material or arguments that have not been discussed in the body of the essay.

Useful phrases that can be used to trigger critical thinking in your essay (and not just in the conclusion) include:

- On the other hand …
- However, …
- Despite this, …
- Nevertheless …
- The most significant point …
- In the short term …, but in the longer term …
- The most important argument …
- The least effective argument …
- The most important point …
- The magnitude of the effect …
- It depends on …

In some subjects, such as History and Business Management, it is suitable and acceptable in the conclusion to include unanswered questions that have occurred as a result of the research. It is then acceptable to briefly explain why these additional questions may be worthy of further study.

COMMON MISTAKE

Students often include thoughts or ideas in the conclusion that are not relevant to the research question. This simply weakens the value of the analysis in the essay and so limits the candidate's ability to gain marks for critical thinking.

CHAPTER SUMMARY KEY POINTS

- Assessment Criterion C (critical thinking) is worth the most number of marks.

- Taking a critical approach to writing the EE requires you to display the skills of analysis and evaluation.

- Avoid writing essays that are wholly or mainly narrative or descriptive as such essays do not show evidence of analysis, evaluation and critical thinking.

- Any source can contain bias or inaccuracies, so good researchers should question all their research materials.

- Avoid unjustified and subjective comments. Ensure you back up your reasoning and provide evidence to support your judgements.

EXPERT TIP

Refer to the subject-specific advice in the IB *Extended Essay Guide* for further advice on how to show evidence of critical thinking in your chosen subject area.

■ END OF CHAPTER QUIZ

	Question	True	False
1	Critical thinking accounts for the highest number of marks under the assessment criteria for the EE.	■	■
2	Being a critical thinker requires you to question everything (in a constructive manner), rather than taking things at face value.	■	■
3	Essays that are mainly descriptive in nature can be awarded high marks.	■	■
4	You should use reputable, reliable and representative sources.	■	■
5	Evaluation should not be integrated throughout the EE but written separately at the end of the essay.	■	■
6	Essays that are descriptive in nature do not score highly.	■	■
7	Personal views must be backed up by well-reasoned arguments and supported by the evidence presented in the essay.	■	■
8	You can introduce new materials and issues in the conclusion to provide alternative perspectives.	■	■
9	Your evaluation, judgements and conclusion must be consistent with the discussion presented and backed up by evidence.	■	■
10	Your evaluation should appear as a separate section at the end of the essay.	■	■

Base your research question on an <u>issue</u> rather than a <u>subject</u>.

Start from an issue of contemporary global significance rather than subject choice.

What is your local connection?
What is your global connection?

Explore the issue of global significance through a local study.

The six World Studies Extended Essay themes:

- Culture, language and identity
- Conflict, peace and security
- Environmental and/or economic sustainability
- Equality and inequality
- Health and development
- Science, technology and society.

Extended Essay

Use two IB Diploma Programme subjects.

Adopt an interdisciplinary approach.

What are the economic causes of people becoming migrants?	What are the historical factors behind a group of people becoming migrants and being forced from their homes?
What are the economic costs to a country receiving migrants/refugees?	What are the historical conditions that make one nation more or less likely to accept refugees?
Economics	History

Example Topic: The impact of the European refugee and migrant crisis as a consequence of the Syrian Civil War

Reflect on global consciousness.

Global understanding – the ability to think and act in open-minded and intelligent ways about issues of global and local importance.

Global self – a clear idea of yourself as a global citizen but also a member of a local community, a city or a nation, who is able to make a worthwhile contribution to the world.

Global sensitivity – sensitivity to local issues and experiences as part of broader ideas.

9 The World Studies Extended Essay

The World Studies Extended Essay (WSEE)

An increasing number of students who write an Extended Essay (EE) for the IB Diploma are choosing to tackle a question in the area of 'World Studies'. This is an appealing option for students with an interest in contemporary global issues and for those who do not wish to focus on a single IB Diploma subject. However, you and your supervisor should be aware that there are some very specific requirements for the WSEE – a failure to be aware of these could lead to a very disappointing grade!

The WSEE is different to all other EE choices in several ways, because it is:

■ An in-depth interdisciplinary study of an issue of contemporary significance

■ An option for you to conduct an investigation in which you integrate knowledge and modes of thinking from two disciplines

■ An essay that is designed to develop global consciousness (see below) which consists of three capabilities: global sensitivity, global understanding and global self

■ An essay with a chosen topic which must address both an issue of global significance, and requires an interdisciplinary approach.

You are expected to:

■ Adopt an interdisciplinary approach using two IB Diploma Programme subjects.

■ Start from an issue of contemporary global significance rather than subject choice. This means your research question will be based on an issue rather than a subject.

■ Explore the issue of global significance through a local study (see advice below).

■ Reflect on global consciousness.

Global consciousness means:

■ **global sensitivity** – sensitivity to local issues and experiences as part of broader ideas

■ **global understanding** – the ability to think and act in open-minded and intelligent ways about issues of global and local importance

■ **global self** – a clear idea of yourself as a global citizen but also a member of a local community, a city or a nation, who is able to make a worthwhile contribution to the world.

Sensitive, aware and globally minded young people have great value to society and the IB Diploma qualification is uniquely placed to help develop and foster such qualities. The WSEE provides a great opportunity for you to develop as a fully rounded, internationally aware citizen with a clear grasp of global contemporary issues rooted in a local context.

The World Studies Extended Essay is concerned with issues of global consciousness

Transdisciplinary skills are an essential component of the World Studies Extended Essay

---

EXPERT TIP

The Researcher's Reflection Space (RRS) is especially useful when writing a WSEE because it gives you an opportunity to develop your global consciousness. The RRS (see Chapter 7) is where moments of such development are recorded and should help you to reflect upon and deepen your personal connections to the problems under study. You should also gain an insight into how learning about contemporary world issues shapes your values, beliefs and commitments at this formative stage of your life. The very best examples of reflection will reveal your thoughts about who you are as a local, regional and global citizen.

■ What is 'transdisciplinary'?

The WSEE is required to be *transdisciplinary* which means that it should be clearly connected with *two* IB subjects. These have to be approved IB subjects, so subjects such as accounting, engineering, law or education don't qualify. One of the qualifying subjects must be examined in depth and so should probably be a subject that you study at Higher Level. The second subject is subsidiary and covered in less detail though it is vitally important that both subjects are considered adequately. The essay should clearly identify which two subjects are being tackled and frequent mention must be made of how the subjects relate to the topic being researched.

The IB suggests that these two subjects should be *disparate* – in other words, it is usually more effective to choose two subjects that are not in the same IB group. Most students choose Group 3 subjects for the WSEE, but it is likely to be more profitable for you to choose Maths and Visual Arts or English and Geography than History with Psychology. This is because it is more likely that you will make clear use of both subjects if they are dissimilar. Ideally your supervisor in a WSEE will be a specialist in the main subject, though this is not always possible in every school. In any case, the student who writes such an essay may also have to consult with an expert in the subsidiary subject at times. As a minimum, the IB recommends that your supervisor for the WSEE should be suitably qualified to give you advice in at least one of the two chosen subjects.

There are six WSEE themes which are part of the registration process when your EE Coordinator or IB Coordinator registers your essay with the IBO. Your WSEE must fit into one of these six categories:

■ Culture, language and identity

■ Conflict, peace and security

■ Environmental and/or economic sustainability

■ Equality and inequality

■ Health and development

■ Science, technology and society.

Note: these are not World Studies subjects but *themes*. In other words, the WSEE reverses the normal principle of EE choice since with a subject EE you should choose the subject first and then the topic but with a WSEE it is the other way round.

> **EXPERT TIP**
>
> When choosing your WSEE research question you will need to think carefully about the following three issues:
>
> ● What is your local connection?
>
> ● What is your global connection?
>
> ● What are your two subject areas?
>
> If you don't have a clear answer to these, you are unlikely to write a good WSEE!

■ What is 'local'?

You must be aware that the WSEE should be concerned with an issue of *global* importance. This should not be too difficult to identify but it should also be explained and demonstrated by a *local* example. This can simply be *localized*. In other words, it does not have to be concerned with the area where you live, although local studies often provide the best opportunity for collection of unique and ingenious data, such as in-depth interviews and quality surveys.

'Local' is quite flexible because it could refer to a small village or a country. The point is that you are able to make the connection between what is happening at a local level and the global theme under which you are submitting your essay. The ideas for many essays originate from students' involvement in activities in their local communities, often as part of Creativity, Activity and Service (CAS) opportunities, or equally from an issue that may have been raised in one of your lessons.

Local does not have to be interpreted as 'local' when writing the essay either. You may live in one country but be concerned by something that is happening in another country. In other words, your issue is one that is local to the population that it is being examined. So, for example, a study of the world refugee crisis would be a suitable *global* study for the WSEE and an examination of the particular problems created by the Syrian Civil War would provide a good *localized* study. However, if the researcher lived in Germany and looked at the impact at home of a large influx of refugees and migrants, this would provide opportunity for a *local* study.

The requirement for the study of a WSEE is that it is based on a topic of contemporary, global significance. This means that the subject-specific interpretations (such as the ten-year rule for History and the five-year rule for Economics) are not applicable to the WSEE.

A World Studies Extended Essay candidate is required to consider a global issue but in a local context.

The World Studies subject-specific guidance (page 367 onwards in the IB *Extended Essay Guide*) should be an area of reference for you and your supervisor.

■ Writing the introduction

Most WSEE students will make clear mention of the two subjects being considered in the introduction to the essay. The introduction of a WSEE is another area where this style of essay differs markedly from a subject-specific EE. Traditional EE introductions are short and structured – they should have:

- A clear statement of the research question
- A section dealing with the significance of the topic, and
- The methods used in the research and writing of the essay.

The introduction in a WSEE should have much more to deal with, so will be longer in length than traditional EEs. The introduction of the WSEE should address questions, such as:

- What is the contemporary global issue being considered?
- Why is this global issue of importance?
- How is this manifested in a local context?
- What subjects form the basis of the WSEE and how do they relate to the research question?
- What methods have been used?
- What is the significance of your research question?

An explanation of how your research question requires an interdisciplinary approach will be very clear if you have written a good introduction. You should also state which IB Diploma Programme subjects will be used and why, and provide some definitions of key concepts selected from these subjects. Don't include irrelevant background material in the introduction, though it is a good idea to write a broad outline of your essay.

■ Research and question choice

If you've decided to write a WSEE, you'll need to choose your interdisciplinary research area and your research question. Interdisciplinary research can be both exciting and complex.

As with a subject-based Extended Essay, your choice of research question in a World Studies Extended Essay is very important

It is exciting because it enables you to:

- Tackle questions that are interesting to you without having to restrict yourself to a single discipline or inquiry approach
- Uncover original and unexpected findings that can only be seen when disciplines are combined.

It is challenging because it requires you to:

- Examine your different topics of study very carefully
- Select information from a broad variety of disciplines and subject areas
- Connect insights in informed and imaginative ways.

Choosing a topic

There are many interesting topics that are potentially suitable for a WSEE. The following table highlights some questions that should guide you in your choice of a suitable topic.

It has personal connection

Is the topic something that you find interesting or that matters to you? Why do you want to know more about it?	Most likely, but not necessarily, you will want to research an issue related to the community or country in which you live.

It is multifaceted

Does the topic require you to look at more than one subject in order to really understand it? How will these subjects come together to help you answer your research question?	You should select a topic or issue that naturally invites the attention of different subjects and invites multiple perspectives.

It is contemporary and of global significance

Does researching this question help you to understand not just your own community/country, but also other countries and/or the world?	While the issues you investigate may be rooted in your local context, you should focus on something that helps you understand the wider globalized world in which you live and that addresses an issue of relevance to people living in different contexts.

It is viable

Will you be able to find the necessary experts, data, information and resources to really understand the topic? Is there enough time to complete this and within 4,000 words?	As with all EEs, the scope of the topic must be manageable, particularly as you will be drawing from more than one subject in the WSEE.

■ Finding a topic of personal interest

Write out a list of issues that you care about or would like to know more about. You can use categories, such as politics, economics, science, environment, society, media, equality, inequality, art, language and culture to help you.

Imagine you were going to contribute some of your own money, or raise funds for a good cause – who would you give the money to and why would that be your choice? Don't limit your ideas to just charity organizations – research institutions, for example, might be doing work that you think is important, or maybe non-governmental groups are involved in a cause that you find worthwhile. These considerations, if they are of personal interest, should be pursued.

■ Finding a contemporary topic of global significance

Browse through a selection of local, national and international newspapers or journals. You can make clippings or take notes of themes (of interest to you) that seem important both on a local and an international level.

Write out ideas that come to your mind when you see the word 'globalization' or the slogan 'think global, act local'. What themes emerge for you?

Interview some adults you know, particularly those who grew up in the place you live in now. How do they think life has changed since they were your age? What concerns them or intrigues them about what is happening in the world today, and how do they see this issue affecting the area in which you live?

■ Finding a topic with different layers and approaches

Think about how your topic could be approached from different IB Diploma Programme subjects. Then see if there are any interesting connections that you can draw between these different subjects.

See below for an idea of how to set out different concepts and get ideas on a topic.

What are the economic causes of people becoming migrants?	What are the historical factors behind a group of people becoming migrants and being forced from their homes?
What are the economic costs to a country receiving migrants/refugees?	What are the historical conditions that make one nation more or less likely to accept refugees?

Economics	History

Topic: The impact of the European refugee and migrant crisis as a consequence of the Syrian Civil War.

TASK 1

Draw out the table below and have a go at filling in the boxes with questions regarding Religion and Human rights, using two different subjects of your choice.

Questions regarding religion and human rights	

Subject 1:	Subject 2:

Topic:

Possible connections from the table might include:

- How have religious leaders and religious practices affected how people in different societies make choices about their lives?
- What are the implications of my findings for refugee policy in Europe? (Makes connections between World Religions and History or Global Politics).
- Which countries (if any) are providing access to refugee/migrant care as a human right and why?
- How could such treatment be extended and made economically viable to more people?
- How has the literature and writing of refugees and others impacted on perceptions of the refugee crisis?
- How are news and media reports important in affecting our understanding and perceptions of refugees and war?

You should now have three or four possible topics and will need to narrow this down to just one or two for your first conversation with your supervisor.

Use a table like this to help with the process of narrowing down to a final, clear choice of topic.

Questions	Option 1	Option 2	Option 3	Option 4
Which topic do I feel most connected to? Which do I care most about?	☐	☐	☐	☐
Which topic seems most relevant for understanding today's interconnected and globalized world?	☐	☐	☐	☐
Which topic seems to offer the most compelling and interesting reason for bringing perspectives from different subjects together?	☐	☐	☐	☐
Which topic seems most feasible in terms of available time, resources and expertise?	☐	☐	☐	☐

Now you are ready to start! Your research question might not be perfect at first and it may change and alter a little over time. This is very normal and is part of the intellectual process of writing an academic research paper. You should however by now have a fairly clear idea of where you are going with the essay and what your title question is likely to be.

> **EXPERT TIP**
>
> As you will need to cover two subjects, one of which you may not be studying, make sure you gain access to the subject syllabuses. Your supervisor or EE Coordinator will be able to help you with this.

■ Avoiding weak World Studies Extended Essay questions

It is important to think not only about what would make a strong question in World Studies, but what would make a weak one. This will help make sure that the question you write is a good one. A weak WSEE question is one that:

- Does not give a strong sense of why the inquiry is important
- Fails to link with a global issue

- Does not illustrate why the research question is important

- Is too broad and cannot be answered properly in 4,000 words

- Is based too much on common sense or obvious information and, especially, relies too much on information from the internet

Don't let your World Studies Extended Essay question be a weak one!

- Does not make it clear how the IB subjects are related to the inquiry or how they are linked together

- Has a focus on a global issue but the essay only draws on one subject discipline

- Is descriptive and narrative, that is, does not analyze or critically examine the global issue that is being studied

- Has a focus that is interdisciplinary but where the research question does not address a global issue.

So, writing an EE in World Studies offers some very unique challenges and problems, but these challenges also offer some exciting possibilities for your intellectual growth.

EXPERT TIP

It pays to read the examiner reports when considering how best to approach a WSEE. Typically, the reports suggest the following main areas of concern:

- Too much emphasis on current news media instead of academic sources, such as academic journals

- A failure to make clear mention of the two IB subjects covered

- Failure to mention the local manifestation of the global study

- Insufficient analysis and evaluation of the sources used.

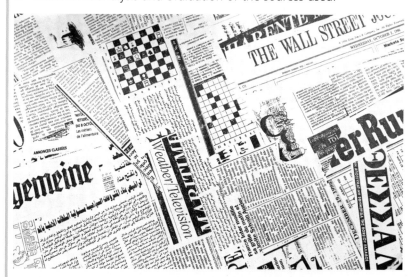

Don't rely too much on current news media or the internet for your sources

EXPERT TIP

The Researcher's Reflection Space (see Chapter 7) is an effective way of demonstrating insight and understanding as you make progress throughout the process of completing your WSEE.

Good World Studies Extended Essay research questions

The choice of question when writing a WSEE is just as important as when writing a subject-specific EE. Things for you to consider include:

1 Can two different IB Diploma Programme subjects be considered to address the research question?

2 Are they concerned with/interested in a global issue within a localized context?

3 Do the questions have a narrow and specific focus so that the topic can be properly covered within the word limit?

Consider the suitability of the following questions:

- 'To what extent have media reports on the recent refugee problem in Syria made the crisis worse?'

- 'To what extent is the current refugee crisis a consequence of British and French decisions in the partition of the Middle East in 1919?'

- 'To what extent is the treatment of refugees in Asia different to Europe due to humanitarian, economic or culture issues?'

TASK 2

Good or bad?

Copy the table below and decide whether each of these WSEE questions are good or bad. Try to explain **why** you think it's good or bad.

	Research question
1	What are the economic and human rights factors that promote and or hinder the success of the US health care system?
2	What is the role of food preparation and eating methods in rural India in relationship to the development of stomach disorders?
3	What social and cultural impact would the closing of the Public Libraries in East London have on the community?
4	To what extent is rainforest destruction the result of development, and is this process necessary for the growth of the Republic of Ecuador?
5	To what extent does the modern European fashion industry influence traditional Middle Eastern culture?
6	Is France's ban on burkas an infringement on human rights? A case for and against such a ban.
7	The alienation of youth in urban Britain.
8	What is the present form of press control in China and what is its history?
9	What are the most appropriate public health and social policies needed to address the causes of obesity in Australia?
10	The use of social networking in promoting education in remote rural areas.

Links to TOK

- How do we know that an issue is of 'global significance'?
- How do we measure the significance of a global issue – is the geographical spread more important or should we measure significance by the number of people who are directly affected?
- To what extent is our opinion of what is significant affected by how 'newsworthy' an event is?

CHAPTER SUMMARY KEY POINTS

- The WSEE is becoming increasingly popular.

- It is an interdisciplinary essay, with direct links to two IB Diploma Programme subjects.

- The WSEE provides you with the opportunity to write an EE on a contemporary issue of global significance within a local context.

- When formulating your WSEE research question, think carefully about: your local connection, your global connection, and your two chosen Diploma Programme subjects.

- The WSEE is likely to have a much longer introduction than a traditional EE.

- Your choice of sources is important. Use academic sources and don't rely too much on current news media or the internet.

- There are six themes for the WSEE and your essay must fall into one of these.

- A good WSEE research question will consider: a global issue within a localized context, two IB Diploma Programme subject disciplines and a narrow focus to enable the essay to be successfully completed within 4,000 words.

■ END OF CHAPTER QUIZ

	Question	True	False
1	A WSEE is interdisciplinary and must be approached from the perspective of two subjects.	☐	☐
2	The two subjects can be any academic discipline.	☐	☐
3	The WSEE must have a local context.	☐	☐
4	The WSEE is unique in that it requires an interdisciplinary study, so the normal word limit of 4,000 words does not apply.	☐	☐
5	Subject-specific rules, such as the ten-year rule for History do not apply to the WSEE.	☐	☐
6	The introduction in the WSEE is usually expected to be longer than that of a subject-based EE.	☐	☐
7	You don't have to be studying both subjects that you choose to form the basis of your transdisciplinary WSEE.	☐	☐
8	You must base your WSEE on more than two subjects to ensure it is interdisciplinary.	☐	☐
9	You may have two supervisors for the WSEE as it is interdisciplinary.	☐	☐
10	It is often better if the two subjects you choose are from different IB Diploma groups.	☐	☐

Understand the requirements

- Assessment criteria.
- Research question.
- Formal presentation (for example, word limit, citations and referencing).
- An uploaded RPPF.

Get started

- The Extended Essay process is about **40 hours** in duration.
- It's a marathon rather than a sprint, so pace yourself and take regular breaks.
- Avoid the demotivation cycle!
- Take control of time, rather than allowing time to take control of you.

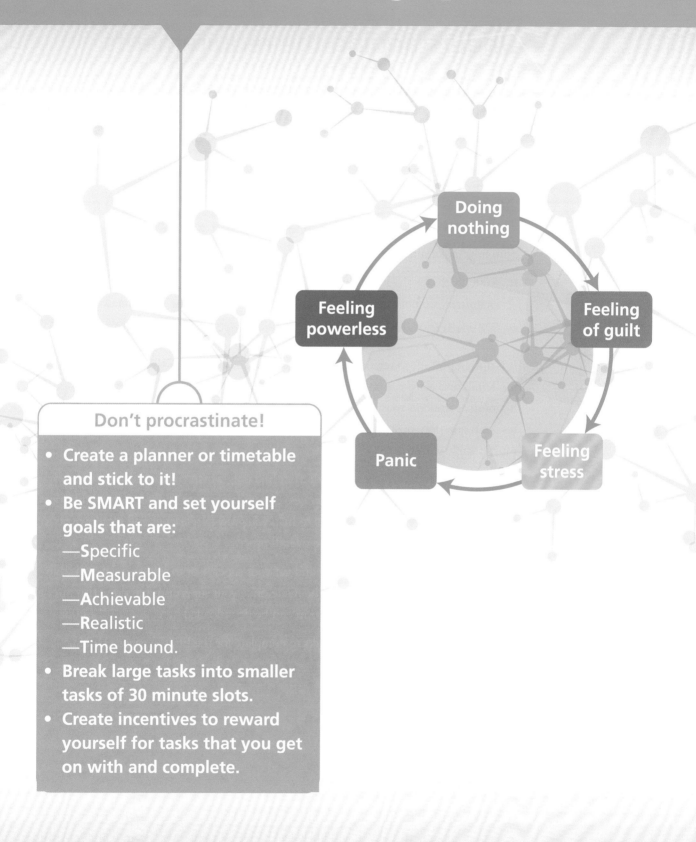

Doing nothing

Feeling powerless

Feeling of guilt

Panic

Feeling stress

Don't procrastinate!

- **Create a planner or timetable and stick to it!**
- **Be SMART and set yourself goals that are:**
  —**Specific**
  —**Measurable**
  —**Achievable**
  —**Realistic**
  —**Time bound.**
- **Break large tasks into smaller tasks of 30 minute slots.**
- **Create incentives to reward yourself for tasks that you get on with and complete.**

10 Managing the Extended Essay process

Understanding the requirements

This book has explained the various requirements of the Extended Essay (EE), from its formal presentation to understanding the assessment criteria. Make sure you are familiar with the formal requirements of the EE, be it about the type of research question asked, the word limit or the use of citations and referencing.

It is important to remember to include proper citation and referencing (see Chapter 5) throughout your essay. Not only is this a requirement for academic honesty reasons, it also shows respect for the ideas and work of other people.

Similarly, make sure you understand and stick to the word limits:

- 4,000 words for the EE (essays in excess of 4,000 words are subject to penalties as examiners are not required to read material in excess of the word limit).
- 500 words for the RPPF (Reflections on Planning and Progress Form).

It is also important to refer to the subject-specific advice in the IB *Extended Essay Guide* for details and clarification of the requirements for your chosen subject. For example, Economics students must adhere to the five-year rule (page *155*) and your Economics research question must not be about an upcoming or theoretical incident. History students must comply with the ten-year rule (page *184*).

Engagement is formally assessed (Criterion E), being worth 6 out of the 34 marks. By genuinely engaging in the EE, the process can become more 'fun' (or purposeful) for you as a learner. Engagement is intended to help you grow as a learner and to allow you to feel proud of what you have learnt in the overall process.

Complete each section of the RPPF and get your supervisor to sign and date this. No other amendments to the form can be made once your supervisor has done this after each reflection session is complete. The form can be downloaded here: goo.gl/ZLLc0o.

For a comprehensive checklist of tasks to complete for the EE, see pages 111–113.

Getting started

The duration of the EE process is about **40 hours**. Getting started means you are taking control of time, rather than allowing time to control you. This will also help to prevent a negative spiral effect on your level of motivation.

The root cause of the problem faced by many IB Diploma students – the demotivation cycle – is doing nothing. You will likely feel better as soon as you begin doing something about your work, while doing nothing means nothing will change. See the section on procrastination below for further guidance on getting started and keeping motivated.

All aspects of the Extended Essay must focus on and relate to the research question

The demotivation cycle

EXPERT TIP

Working on your EE for even just 10 minutes a day will go a long way. We can only get better at the things we do regularly.

Dealing with procrastination

One of the biggest hurdles facing IB Diploma students is how to handle procrastination. We are constantly faced with tempting distractions, such as our smartphones, the urge to check and share updates on social media, and irrationally trying to convince ourselves that 'there is always tomorrow'. However, promising to get things done is not enough to actually get anything done.

Procrastination refers to the psychological barriers that prevent you from working. It is natural and everyone does it to some extent! However, the EE writing process will become much more manageable as soon as you do something about it.

Actions speak louder than words

Smartphones can be a major distractor to work

Try some of these strategies to help you to deal with procrastination:

■ Create a planner and stick to it! Lots of people find it useful to have a 'to do' list or a checklist (see end of this chapter).

■ Try to be SMART in what it is you are trying to achieve – your targets should be:

   □ **S**pecific

   □ **M**easurable

   □ **A**chievable

   □ **R**ealistic

   □ **T**ime bound.

■ Break large tasks into smaller tasks of 30-minute slots. For example, work specifically on the introduction or secondary research rather than trying to tackle too much at a time.

■ Create incentives to reward yourself for tasks that you get on with and complete. Rewards, including fun things to do, are important as they allow you to get more things done (and therefore procrastinate less).

■ Be smarter about your use of time in order to free up some time. For example, can you make better use of 'dead time', such as when travelling to/from school? Is there some reading you can do or a podcast you can listen to which will help with the research or writing process?

■ Use free or paid-for online apps for support. *Forest* (available from iTunes) is an app which temporarily prevents you from accessing websites on your smartphone – this means you have one less thing to distract you! Often apps or websites can be blocked for a pre-determined time, but you still have access to the internet (for work-related matters).

Being able to stay on top of your work relies on your research and time keeping skills as well as your ability to prioritize. These traits will help you at university and your future career too. Essentially, while managing the EE process can take time to plan, it will save you more time in the long run.

Nevertheless, it is important to pace yourself and to take regular breaks. Our brains, like all muscles, need a break too. You could, for example, work for 25 minutes at a time and take a 5-minute break. This helps to reduce procrastination and improves focus and productivity.

EXPERT TIP

To ensure your essay focuses only on the research question, plan your research to directly address the title question.

EXPERT TIP

Remember to use your supervisor for support! Make the most of the opportunities you have to meet your supervisor for support, rather than spend the time procrastinating.

EXPERT TIP

As the essay needs to be electronically uploaded, this will make it easier for examiners to know at which point your EE has reached 4,000 words. Examiners are instructed not to read beyond the word limit. You have been warned!

EXPERT TIP

Supervisors can access a range of resources from the IB's Programme Resource Centre (resources.ibo.org), such as teacher support materials, sample EEs and subject-specific guidance. You should politely ask your supervisor to share these resources with you.

CHAPTER SUMMARY KEY POINTS

- Make sure you are familiar with the formal requirements of the EE.

- There are so many distractions in modern society so you need effective strategies to tackle procrastination (psychological barriers to work).

- Set yourself SMART goals to help you with the planning process.

- Create a planner and stick to it in a rather strict and disciplined way. This will help you to better manage the overall process.

- You should read the subject-specific advice in the IB *Extended Essay Guide* to get details and clarification of the requirements for your chosen Diploma Programme subject.

- You need to complete all the sections of the RPPF and get your supervisor to sign and date this too.

- The duration of the EE process is about 40 hours, so plan and use your time sensibly and productively.

- Your supervisor and EE Coordinator are at hand to help you throughout the overall process.

■ END OF CHAPTER QUIZ

	Question	True	False
1	To score well in the EE, careful planning with reference to the assessment criteria is vital.	☐	☐
2	Procrastination is one of the largest barriers to effective management of the EE.	☐	☐
3	The duration of the EE process is about 50 hours.	☐	☐
4	The use of citation and referencing throughout your essay shows respect for the ideas and work of other people.	☐	☐
5	The supervision process should total three to five hours, which includes the three mandatory reflection sessions.	☐	☐
6	Setting SMART targets can help you to better manage the EE process.	☐	☐
7	Engagement in the EE process helps you to grow as a learner.	☐	☐
8	As the EE needs to be electronically uploaded, you must use Times New Roman or Arial font size 14.	☐	☐
9	Your supervisor must sign and date the RPPF shortly after your reflection meeting and submission of your written reflection.	☐	☐
10	Creating a planner and sticking to it can help you to better manage your EE.	☐	☐

Appendices

Top 10 tips for writing a successful Extended Essay

Top 10 tips from students

1 Start early!

2 Get your title right; your supervisor can help you with this.

3 Spread your work out into manageable tasks.

4 Meet your supervisor regularly – turn up for all the meetings!

5 Stick to all deadlines.

6 Don't leave the citations and referencing until the end of the process as you'll find it near-impossible to compile a decent bibliography.

7 Ask your supervisor for help with the structure and format of the essay.

8 Use a range of secondary sources and avoid source bias.

9 Make sure you write in an objective way – your arguments and conclusion should be derived from the research and evidence presented in the essay.

10 Do not procrastinate – this is the number one reason why students struggle with the EE!

Top 10 tips from the authors

1 Phrase your title as a probing research question that is worthy of study.

2 Conduct thorough and meaningful research. This will help to improve the accuracy of your analysis and help your critical thinking.

3 In order to limit potential source bias, consider the strengths and limitations of your sources. This also helps with providing evidence for critical thinking.

4 Make sure you understand the assessment criteria (see Chapter 1 for further details and guidelines). To score well, you must show evidence of critical thinking.

5 Make sure you understand the subject-specific rules for the EE.

6 Read previous essays to identify strengths and possible limitations in order to improve your own work (but be careful about the rules on academic honesty).

7 Get help from your school Librarian on research and referencing skills for the EE. You can also seek help from your EE Coordinator.

8 Be careful of source bias and question the validity of your research in order to write a meaningful discussion.

9 Pay attention to the three mandatory reflection sessions as these are an integral aspect of the EE (and assessed under Criterion E).

10 It is strongly recommended that you type your essay (if you don't already) as examiners no longer accept hard copies. Handwritten essays or those that include hand-drawn figures/diagrams must be scanned for electronic upload.

Extended Essay Student Checklist

Cover page (Title page)

Have you included the research question?

Have you stated the subject?

Have you included your personal code?

Have you ensured you have kept the cover page anonymous (no candidate name or number and no centre name or centre number)?

Have you declared the word count?

Declaration of authenticity

Have you included a signed declaration of authenticity?

Have you dated the declaration of authenticity?

Have you submitted the declaration of authenticity to your supervisor for safekeeping?

Research question (RQ)

Is your title phrased as a probing question?

Is your RQ clearly stated?

Is the purpose and focus of your RQ clear and appropriate?

Have you outlined why your RQ is worthy of investigation?

Can your RQ be answered in 4,000 words (is it focused rather than too vague)?

Contents page

Have you included a contents page?

Have you used section headings?

Does this include page numbers?

Have you checked the page numbers are accurate?

Methodology

Have you made it clear why your methodology is relevant to the RQ?

Have you outlined how your sources help you answer the RQ?

Have you used a sufficient range of suitable sources?

Is there evidence of informed selection of sources?

Have you used all aspects of the methodology mentioned in the introduction of your essay?

Analysis, discussion and critical thinking

Have you used subject-specific terminology and concepts appropriately, accurately and consistently?

Analysis, discussion and critical thinking

Have you made links between your research findings/data collected and your research question?	☐
Have you explained the significance of the information/data in your essay?	☐
Are your points supported by evidence?	☐
Are your arguments consistent with the analysis and sources presented?	☐
Have you acknowledged the significance of possible errors or omissions that may have occurred in your research?	☐
Have you considered the degree of reliability (strengths and limitations) of your sources?	☐
Have you provided a critical evaluation of the methodologies, data and subject-specific tools used?	☐

Conclusion

Is your research question restated and appears in bold in the conclusion?	☐
Is your conclusion consistent with the discussion provided in the essay?	☐
Have you provided reasoned arguments with relevant evidence to justify your conclusion?	☐
Is your conclusion meaningful and backed by research evidence?	☐
Does your conclusion acknowledge any unresolved questions?	☐
Does your conclusion address new questions that have emerged (if any)?	☐

Reflections

Have you completed all three reflection sessions?	☐
Have you demonstrated engagement with your research question and the research process?	☐
Is there evidence of the thinking process behind any changes in direction in your research and methodology?	☐
Have you highlighted the challenges you faced, and how you overcame these?	☐
Upon completion of the *viva voce*, have you completed your final summative comments, signed and dated the RPPF before submitting this to your supervisor?	☐
Do your reflections highlight the successes in your learning journey?	☐

Format and formal presentation

Is your essay within 4,000 words?	☐
Does your research question appear in bold in the introduction?	☐
Have you used a readable font, such as Arial or Times New Roman?	☐
Is the essay in size 12 font?	☐
Is your essay double-spaced?	☐
Are all of your pages numbered?	☐
Are graphs/charts/images/illustrations numbered?	☐

Format and formal presentation

Are each of your graphs/charts/images/illustrations captioned?	☐
Are your graphs/charts/images/illustrations referenced appropriately?	☐
Are all your diagrams, charts and graphs correctly labelled?	☐
Do the page numbers in your table of contents match the page numbers in the text?	☐
Have you proofread the entire essay for spelling, punctuation and/or grammatical errors?	☐
Is your work anonymized, that is, your candidate name and number do not appear anywhere in the essay?	☐
Have you used a consistent system to cite and reference your sources?	☐
If quotations have been used, have you clearly indicated these (by using quotation marks or an indented paragraph)?	☐
Has the source of each quotation (if used) been cited?	☐
Where you have used the ideas of someone else, have you clearly indicated where this starts and ends?	☐
Does the appendix (if used) contain only relevant and necessary information?	☐
Does each appendix item (if used) have a title *and* an appropriate source?	☐
Are each of the appendix items (if used) clearly mentioned in the text of the essay?	☐
Are all references to items in the appendix clearly cross-referenced, including the relevant page number(s)?	☐

Bibliography (Works cited or References)

Have you included a bibliography, containing all your sources used to research and write the EE?	☐
Has the bibliography been produced in alphabetical order?	☐
Do your citations in the body of the essay match the correct references in the bibliography?	☐
Does your bibliography list each and every source used in the essay?	☐
Does your bibliography specify author(s), title, date of publication and the publisher for every reference?	☐
Is the punctuation in the bibliography consistent?	☐

Others

Have you referred to your RQ throughout the essay (not only in the introduction and conclusion)?	☐
Have you shared a soft copy of the final version of the EE with your supervisor?	☐
Do you have everything ready to submit your completed essay to your supervisor by the final deadline?	☐

Answers

Chapter 1

Quiz

1 True

2 False – The number of assessment criteria has been reduced to 5, but each is worth a different number of marks.

3 True

4 False – The RRS is a recommendation (especially for WSEE students) but not a formal requirement.

5 False – An E grade continues to be a failing condition for the entire IB Diploma.

6 False – The level will be awarded as long as the majority of indicators have been met.

7 True

8 True

9 False – The essay is marked out of a total of 34 points.

10 False – The recommendation is the supervisor spends a minimum of three hours and a maximum of five hours with each candidate.

Chapter 2

Tasks

■ Task 1

The suggested answers below are examples used in History, but the same principles apply to other subjects too.

Higher Level subject	Possible Extended Essay question (phrased as a question) that is unusual, challenging and inventive.
History	'To what extent can it be said that Nazi economic policies of the 1930s were such a failure that they drove Germany into a war they could neither afford or win?'
	'In what ways can it be argued that Deng Xiaoping's reforms in China in the 1980s were of limited success and created more problems than they solved?'
	'How important was the construction and propaganda impact of the Moscow metro in Stalin's consolidation of power after 1935?'

These questions are good and interesting because they challenge preconceived ideas and take an unusual approach to the topic.

■ Task 2

Possible research questions for proposed titles:

■ 'To what extent did Dickens' descriptions of industrial squalor and the urban poor accurately reflect conditions in London in the 1850s and help to create change?'

■ 'Every child must be numerate by the time they leave Primary school' (Gordon Brown, British Prime Minister, 2007)

In what ways can the use of theatre and drama aid the development of numeracy and literacy in the Primary classroom?

Possible title for proposed research question:

- 'Man is still the most extraordinary computer of all' (John F. Kennedy)

Task 3

Essay title number	Good or bad?	Reasons
1	Bad	Far too broad – how is it possible to compare all wars?
2	Bad	Too broad but has potential if certain 'aspects' of the First World War are clarified, for example, medical advances from plastic surgery, prosthetics, flu viruses, bacterial infections or disease control hygiene.
3	Good	Specific and focused, but needs to be stated as a question.
4	Good	Potentially a good question but needs to be more focused and specific (such as the type of comics and/or type of art).
5	Bad	Far too broad – it is impossible to study all heroes in literature over a 2,000-year period!
6	Bad	Needs to be restated as a question and arguably lacks interest.
7	Bad	The topic is too broad and it is not phrased as a question. It is also unclear whether this is an Economics, Business Management, History, Psychology, Design Technology or Biology question.
8	Bad	There is no focus to the study of Pi, so the topic is too broad (especially as the title is not stated as a question). It is unclear whether this is a Mathematics or Computer Science essay. What is the focus and purpose? A terrible 'question'!
9	Good	A good specific question, as long as it is clear which subject discipline (Economics or Business Management?)
10	Good	A good specific Biology question.

Task 4

It's your choice which ones to try, though you'll probably choose one of the questions that are relevant to your HL subjects. Whichever you choose, remember the rules – not too simplistic, not too complicated and phrased as a question. The question should be narrow and specific, otherwise you'll never cover it in 4,000 words – and remember, too, that it must be clearly related to ONE recognized IB Diploma subject (unless it's a WSEE).

Task 5

Though the list is by no means definitive, any focused question that is specific to a single IB subject and uses a wide range of sources is likely to be suitable. Examples of possible research questions include:

- To what extent were Germany's economic misfortunes from 1919 to 1933 the key reason for Hitler's rise to power? (History)

- To what extent is depression caused by one's environment? (Psychology)

- To what extent is it possible to make a valid comparative study of population growth models for country X over the last x years and make future predictions for growth? (Mathematics)

- To what extent has the aesthetic design of the world's tallest buildings been a success? (Visual Arts)

- How has Peter Jackson used generic and narrative structures in his Lord of the Rings movies? (Film)

Task 6

Suggested answers to why the following are *not* good research questions:

- *The origins of the Cold War:* Too descriptive and narrative and would benefit from being restricted to a time frame. Should be phrased as a question.

- *English novels:* Should be phrased as a question. Far too broad and narrative – what aspect of English novels is being considered?

- *How to design a space shuttle:* This should be phrased as a question. Which IB subject does this relate to? It's probably too complicated to be tackled as an EE.

- *Why should we expect a flu epidemic?:* Too broad and general, and this question is based on an assumption that is possibly unprovable.

- *When should we expect the next tsunami?:* A hypothetical question that is nearly impossible to answer, especially without any context. It is better to consider a question related to how scientists are trying to predict future earthquakes and tsunamis.

- *Do Dry Shirts work? How do they work?:* Poorly phrased question and it is not clear which IB subject category this would fit into.

- *Are Chinese medicines effective?:* Too broad a question, and what aspect of Chinese medicine is being considered here? It is not clear what 'effective' refers to and under what circumstances.

- *Was Albert Einstein an atheist?:* A broad and narrative question that is almost impossible to prove.

- *The NBA in China:* Should be phrased as a question, but the topic is much too broad and likely to lead to a narrative essay without any substantiated arguments.

Quiz

1 True

2 True

3 False – This criterion is worth 6 marks; Criterion C is allocated 12 marks.

4 False – It must be specific to one IB subject (unless you are writing a World Studies EE).

5 True

6 False – WSEEs should focus on two recognized IB Diploma subjects.

7 True

8 False – The structure must support the reading, analysis and evaluation of the essay in relation to the research question.

9 True

10 True

Chapter 3

Quiz

1 True

2 True

3 False – Examiners are not required to access external sources or supplementary material.

4 True

5 False – Footnotes and endnotes can only be used for referencing purposes.

6 True

7 False – Any recognized or consistent referencing system would suffice.

8 True

9 False – You need to use your personal code instead.

10 True

Chapter 4

Quiz

1 True

2 False – Allowing a friend to use part of your work is considered academic malpractice.

3 True

4 False – The source must be fully referenced.

5 False – This is academic malpractice.

6 True

7 False – Although this may be encouraged, it is not a requirement.

8 True

9 True

10 False – A school competition or sporting event does not exempt your from the official school deadline.

Chapter 5

Quiz

1 True

2 True

3 True

4 False – The IB expects the use of C&R but does not prescribe a particular system.

5 True

6 True

7 True

8 True

9 False – Both are required.

10 False – The EE Coordinator and Librarian can also help.

Chapter 6

Quiz

1 False – The recommended supervision time is three to five hours.

2 True

3 False – The supervisor is not permitted to edit and annotate at all, though may give feedback and advice on one draft.

4 False – The *viva voce* should last for 20 to 30 minutes.

5 True

6 True

7 True

8 False – All comments on the RPPF must be anonymous.

9 True

10 False – There must be no similarity between two pieces of work submitted by a candidate for the IB Diploma – this is known as 'double dipping' and deemed as academic malpractice.

Chapter 7

Tasks

■ Task 1

1 This is a simple task – what did you do? You don't need to include everything of course (that would take ages!) but what were the highlights and the main things that you did?

2 This is a bit trickier. Think carefully about how you define what was a success and what was not. Getting what you wanted is not necessarily an indicator of success and sometimes it's not possible to really understand if something was successful or went well until a little time afterwards.

3 This is at the heart of 'Reflection'. This is not a task designed to make you beat yourself up or *criticize* yourself too much. Instead it's about personal growth and self-analysis. This is all part of the journey – understanding what you did and why and perhaps considering how you could do things differently and more productively next time.

■ Task 2

Much of this will be guesswork at the start of the process because you have only just started! However, now that you have made some progress on the EE you should have a better idea of what makes a good research question and how to conduct your research. Much of this is trial and error and that's OK – it's all part of the process! It's the same when you write any academic research paper; your question and approach will change as you begin your research – it would be quite surprising if the research question you chose at the start is exactly the same as the one that you eventually use. Part of the reason for this is that your research takes you in a different direction due to what information is available and because of what takes your interest.

All of this should be recorded in the RRS – you'll find this invaluable when you write your RPPF which remember is worth 6 of the total marks!

Quiz

1 True

2 True

3 True

4 False – The RPPF is marked out of 6 and graded by an examiner.

5 True

6 True

7 False – There is a maximum of 500 words (for all three reflections).

8 False – The RRS is a recommendation but not a compulsory element.

9 False – The RPPF cannot be changed after it has been written and submitted.

10 True

Chapter 8

Task

■ Task 1

■ **Possible answers**

1 People naturally assume that Friday is a day in the week (which it is, of course). However, why can't Friday also be a name? Friday is the name of the cowboy's horse!

2 Many people would think this is a very straightforward question (asked by an 8-year old) – the answer is clearly 100. However, a critical thinker would consider that the answer could be a negative number, that is, −999.

3 Again, why can't someone's name be Each? Each is the name of the (only) person that took an apple from the tree.

4 It's daytime! Just because the dog is black and the driver doesn't have his lights on doesn't mean it has to be night-time.

Quiz

1 True

2 True

3 False – Low marks against assessment Criterion C (critical thinking).

4 True

5 False – It's the other way round.

6 True

7 True

8 False – Only any unanswered questions that stemmed from your research.

9 True

10 False – Evaluation should appear throughout the essay.

Chapter 9

Tasks

◼ Task 1

You should have constructed a diagram that is potentially very useful for writing the WSEE. The two subjects you chose are likely to be Group 3 subjects for the purpose of this example, but remember that the best WSEEs are often based around two contrasting subjects from different groups. Remember the two subjects that you choose must be two recognized IB Diploma subjects.

◼ Task 2

1 Bad – Too broad and questionable whether it is a global issue.

2 Bad – Not a very promising question, and could end up being very descriptive. The global issue is not clear either.

3 Bad – Is this really a global issue? It would be difficult to prove cause and effect.

4 Good – As long as a global context is established (environmental depletion, perhaps), this is a good question.

5 Bad – Much too broad; unclear which subjects would be used; not a global issue and a very difficult matter to (dis)prove.

6 Good – Would require critical thinking but a good question if the global issue is established.

7 Bad – Not phrased as a question and unclear which two subjects could be applied.

8 Bad – A descriptive essay, not really a global issue, and not likely to be interdisciplinary.

9 Good – If the topic is placed in global context this question is interdisciplinary and focused.

10 Bad – Not phrased as a question, although there is potential if a local context is recognized.

Quiz

1 True

2 False – The two subjects must be recognized IB Diploma Programme subjects.

3 True

4 False – All EEs written in English have a 4,000-word limit.

5 True

6 True

7 True

8 True

9 False – All EE candidates must have only one supervisor.

10 True

Chapter 10

Quiz

1 True	**6** True
2 True	**7** True
3 False – It is approximately 40 hours.	**8** False – Font size 12.
4 True	**9** True
5 True	**10** True

Index

The Publishers would like to thank the following for permission to reproduce copyright material.

Photo credits

pp.**4–5,14–15,26–27,36–37,48–49,60–61,70–71,82–83,92–93,104–105** © teerayuttae/Fotolia, **p.7** *tl* © dipego/Shutterstock.com, *tr* © lexaarts/Shutterstock.com; **p.8** *tl* © Oleg Ponomarenko/123RF, *tr* © Happymay/Shutterstock.com, *bl* © shaffandi /123RF; **p.10** © Dmitriy Shironosov/123RF; **p.12** © Vadim Guzhva/123RF; **p.16** © Patrick Lienin/123RF; **p.17** © Katsiaryna Lenets/123RF; **p.19** © piccaya/123RF; **p.23** *l* © Patryk Kosmider – Fotolia, *r* © filmfoto / Alamy Stock Photo **p.28** © Jennifer Huls/123RF; **p.29** © BatsGraphic/Shutterstock.com; **p.31** © Dmitrii Kiselev/123RF; **p.34** © Diana Johanna Velasquez/123RF; **p.39** © luckybusiness/123RF; **p.43** © Ana Blazic Pavlovic/123RF; **p.44** © Sirawit hengthabthim/123RF; **p.46** © Tommy E Trenchard/Alamy Stock Photo; **p.51** *tr* © Paul Mann/123RF; **p.53** © juliatim/123RF; **p.57** © Rabia Elif Aksoy/123RF; **p.63** © pixelheadphoto digitalskillet/Shutterstock.com; **p.65** © thelightwriter/123RF; **p.72** © Daniil Peshkov/123RF; **p.73** *tl* © phipatbig/Shutterstock.com, *tr* © bowie15/123RF, *bm* © Oleksandr Brylov/123RF, **p.74** © Ion Chiosea/123RF; **p.77** © Cathy Yeulet/123RF; **p.84** © rawpixel/123RF; **p.86** *tr* © Vanessa van Rensburg/123RF, © vintagevectors/123RF, © diego matteo muzzini/123RF, © bonzami emmanuelle/123RF, *b* © marcos calvo mesa/123RF; **p.87** *bl* © Wiki Commons, *br* © Fletcher & Baylis/Science Photo Library; **p.95** *tl* © 1xpert/123RF, *tr* © Nattanit Pumpuang/123RF; **p.97** © naruedom yaempongsa/123RF; **p.98** © multirealism/123RF; **p.101** © Sergio Barrios/123RF; **p.107** *t* © rawpixel/123RF, *b* © fabio formaggio/123RF.

t = top, *b* = bottom, *c* = centre, *l* = left, *r* = right

Acknowledgements

Every effort has been made to trace all copyright holders, but if any have been inadvertently overlooked, the Publishers will be pleased to make the necessary arrangements at the first opportunity.

Although every effort has been made to ensure that website addresses are correct at time of going to press, Hodder Education cannot be held responsible for the content of any website mentioned in this book. It is sometimes possible to find a relocated web page by typing in the address of the home page for a website in the URL window of your browser.